TEXTILE
—ARTS—
Multicultural Traditions

Margo Singer and Mary Spyrou

Published in 2000 by Davis Publications, Inc.
50 Portland Street, Worcester, MA 01608, USA
by arrangement with A & C Black (Publishers),
35 Bedford Row, London WC1R 4JH, UK

Copyright © 1989 Margo Singer and Mary Spyrou

ISBN 87192–522–2

Printed in Great Britain
at the Bath Press, Bath

TEXTILE
—ARTS—
Multicultural Traditions

Contents

Illustrations

Colour plates

Black and white photographs of finished work

Acknowledgements

Work by the following textile artists is illustrated in this book:

Amira Ahmed, from Karachi, Pakistan
Shahnaz Aslam, from Karachi, Pakistan; dressmaker
Rushton Aust, from Oxford, England; teacher
Janet Bolton, from Lancashire, England
Etha Brandon, from Sierra Leone; teacher
Steve Brockett, from Wales; kite maker
Kathleen Cadle, from Lancashire, England
Noel Dyrenforth, from London; teacher
Aquela Feroz, from Kabul, Afghanistan; teacher
Pat Hodson, from Sheffield, England
Poonam Peswani, from Bombay, India
Julia Pullen, from Yorkshire, England
Sarah Satchell, from Essex, England
Margo Singer, from Manchester, England; teacher
Mary Spyrou, Greek Cypriot from London; teacher
Beatrice Williams, Guyanese/Welsh from Bangor, Wales; teacher
Sue Jones, from New Zealand

Photography by Helen Pask

Line drawings by Dave Farrell

Other material has been supplied for photography by:

Tasneem Raja – from Quetta, Baluchistan, Pakistan, now a teacher (Baluchistan dress for embroidery chapter)
Moira Broadbent – lived in India and Pakistan for twenty-nine years, Fellow of the Society of Designer Craftsmen (animal regalia for embroidery and appliqué chapters)
Liz Nuñez-Perez – lived on the island of Mamitupu, San Blas, Panama (contemporary mola work for appliqué chapter)
Kate Dean and Sally Coombes (modern batiks and tjap cloths for batik chapter)

Photographs have been supplied by:

Chile Solidarity Campaign, London (protest pictures for the appliqué chapter)

Jennie Spyrou (sources of inspiration for designing chapter)

The Lady Richmond Brown Collection at the British Museum, Department of Ethnography (molas for appliqué chapter)

The Charles Beving Collection at the British Museum, Department of Ethnography (for tie and dye and batik chapters)

Platt Hall Museum of Costume, Manchester (examples of nineteenth-century costume for decorative techniques chapter)

Preface

We first became interested in writing a book on textiles while working on a decorative textiles project in the East End of London. The course was largely attended by local Asian women, of Bangladeshi, Pakistani, Indian and Afghan origin. As the project progressed we were impressed by the wealth of skills already possessed by the women; most of them had a vocabulary of hand embroidery stitches taught to them by their mothers and grandmothers, to which they were quickly able to add the machining techniques demonstrated to them on the course. In time they produced rich, exuberant embroidery that included techniques such as quilting, appliqué, reverse appliqué and cutwork.

We later decided to do some research among other ethnic community groups to find out what traditional textile skills were being practised elsewhere in Britain. To our delight we discovered many groups and individuals producing beautiful work. Some were using traditional skills learned in their country of origin but were adapting them to the conditions and particular economy of this country. Others were blending their own methods and style of design with what they were learning of current Western styles – and creating an exciting fusion of both.

The groups and individuals we came across – mostly women – included West Africans and Afro-Caribbeans involved in the crafts of tie and dye, tritik and batik, Asian women producing various styles of shalwar kameez, and Greek Cypriots practising cutwork. We were fascinated by the range of different techniques and design sources used by these groups and individual craftspeople and became interested in recording the information we were rapidly accumulating. We decided to write a textile book based on our diverse experiences.

We selected embroidery, appliqué, tie and dye, batik and various decorative techniques as our focus because such techniques are versatile and relatively simple to use. They require only basic materials to produce a range of colourful abstract or figurative designs – from the geometric to animals, people and flowers – which can be applied to dress, accessories, wall hangings and soft furnishings. We added a brief geographical, historical and cultural survey of the important role of textiles in particular societies.

We want to offer all craftspeople and artists an opportunity to share in these textile traditions and to learn something about the cultures in which the traditions grew up. We hope that this book will encourage people to preserve and treasure what is left of traditional textiles, and to experiment with the techniques described in order to create their own.

Perhaps this will help readers appreciate hand crafted textiles in these days of ever-increasing industrialisation and mass production which are evident globally in the late twentieth century.

The book is also intended to provide a useful source of reference for all those currently involved in organising classroom and workshop activities in multicultural art and craft education – for teachers and students as well as for practising artists and craftspeople.

We should like to extend our thanks to the many friends whose help made this book possible, by the loan of finished work, by their knowledge and experience and, in general, by providing tremendous hospitality while we were compiling the book. Particular acknowledgements are made on another page.

Margo Singer
Mary Spyrou

1 Embroidery

Introduction

Decorating materials with embroidery is an ancient tradition and reveals much to us about the lives and customs of particular cultures.

In prehistoric times man used bone, bronze and thorn for needles and grasses, animal sinew and fibres for thread. Grasses were also interlaced, preceding the practice of spinning wool and hair for weaving. Woven linen is the earliest known fabric. It is believed that the use of darning and simple running stitches to mend, strengthen and ornament led to the early use of embroidery. Textiles developed most rapidly and fully in regions of the world crossed by great rivers: the Nile, Ganges and Euphrates. Cotton and flax were grown in Egypt and cotton in India; silk and gold were brought along the Silk Road from China.

The earliest examples of embroidery date back to 5000 B.C. They are evident in the wall paintings at Luxor in Egypt and fragments show evidence of the use of half cross stitch, darning, weaving, basket and satin stitches. Appliqué and stitched fragments have also been found at Mohenjo Daro, a centre of the Indus Valley Civilisation of Northern India and Pakistan that dates back to 5000 B.C. – an area rich in cotton production. The earliest example of double running stitch was found in a Russian tomb of between A.D. 400 and 500. It appears in a Coptic pattern of Arab or Byzantine influence. A wealth of fabrics (leather, silk, felt and linen) came to light in the Frozen tombs of Pazyryk in the Altai Mountains of Central Asia. They date back to the period of A.D. 350 to 550.

In Europe, the Church was an early exponent of embroidery skills. In the Middle Ages, convents, courts, households and organised craft guilds were well established. There was a trade in European-produced textiles and the importing of more exotic ones from India and beyond. The Bayeux Tapestry was made in 1077 to depict the Battle of Hastings. It is made of wool on linen and consists of laid couched stitches. It was common at the time to embroider military images such as heraldic badges, coats of arms and clothing.

By the end of the fifteenth century embroidered samplers were being made as 'pattern books' of popular stitches (including satin, running and cross stitch) worked on linen. Cross-stitch samples became very popular in the eighteenth and nineteenth centuries, latterly in schools. Patterns included verses, houses, animals, numbers and the alphabet, worked as monochrome and polychrome designs. During this period, convents and missions were being established in India, North America and the Pacific islands. This encouraged the spread of European styles of embroidery and the encounter with local skills.

Nowadays technology has advanced so much that embroidery designs can be swiftly created on domestic sewing machines or on large computer-assisted machinery. The combination of machine and hand embroidery techniques can create an infinite variety of design and texture.

The Embroidery Departments of art and fashion colleges have done much to promote and develop embroidery in new and exciting ways, establishing it as an important art form. Fashion designers now explore its possibilities when creating luxurious fabrics for evening and bridal wear and decorative features for everyday clothing. Sportswear has adopted the use of embroidered motifs on both clothing and accessories.

Embroidery stitches

It is advisable to use embroidery rings (or tambours) which come in a variety of sizes. Have available a selection of embroidery (crewel) needles, silk and cotton threads and fabrics. If you are using embroidery rings, stretch your fabric evenly. Sometimes it is a good idea to bind one ring with fine strips of fabric, tape or ribbon. This will prevent the fabric from being damaged.

Remember to secure a knot at the end of your thread to prevent your embroidery from becoming undone.

Running stitch

This simple stitch can be worked quickly. Several stitches at a time can be made by inserting the needle in and out of the fabric at regular (*1:1*) or irregular intervals. A variation of running stitch is double running stitch where the first row is worked and the second row is worked back over the first row, so that the stitching looks exactly the same on both sides of the fabric. Double running stitch can be executed on a slant to form a zigzag pattern. Closely worked running stitches, commonly called double darning stitch, can be used for infilling shapes.

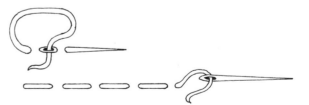

1:1 Running stitch.

Chain stitch

This stitch is used for outlining, infilling and making parallel lines. You can use a needle or a hook. The latter technique is known as tambour work.

To do needle chain stitch, thread your needle with single thread, insert it from underneath the fabric, bring it through and insert again close to where the thread emerges, pushing the point of the needle under and along until it pierces the fabric again (*1:2*). Wind the loop of thread you have made round the tip of the needle and draw the needle through the loop (*1:3*). Repeat.

1:2 Chain stitch.

1:3 Chain stitch.

Variations of needle chain stitch include open chain stitch, made up of open loops achieved by inserting the needle at a slant, and double chain stitch by alternating the needle from left to right. The Irish Cornelli is an electric sewing machine which produces a continuous chain stitch, covering large areas very quickly. It requires a lot of skill to control.

For tambour work in Europe, a fine steel hook is used, often with beadwork. In Gujurat, India, Mochi craftsmen use a hooked awl called an ari which produces a regular stitch. The chain stitch is firstly worked on a very soft leather which is then backed by a sturdier leather. The hook pulls the thread through the fabric from underneath to form the stitch above. Dense patterns can be achieved. Brightly coloured chain stitched shoes in pink, orange, blue, green, white and yellow are commonly worn in Rajasthan, in the northwest. The shoes (*1:4*) are from Jaisalmer in Rajasthan.

1:4 Embroidered slippers from Rajasthan, India.

Satin stitch

Satin stitch is used for filling in all kinds of shapes. Evenly worked in close parallel stitches, it can also be woven to fill in a shape, thereby creating many shades and this is called shaded satin stitch. In this case the minimum of thread is left on the back of the fabric. See *1:31* on page 27.

Illus. *1:5* shows satin stitch used to fill in a geometric shape. Using single thread and starting from the left, make even stitches increasing in width as you move along the shape to the centre, then decreasing. Try and keep your stitches close and flat as this will create a smooth and shiny effect.

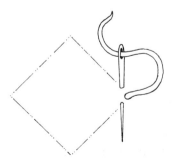
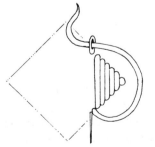
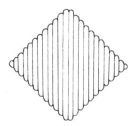

1:5 Satin stitch.

Lazy daisy stitch
See *1:6*.

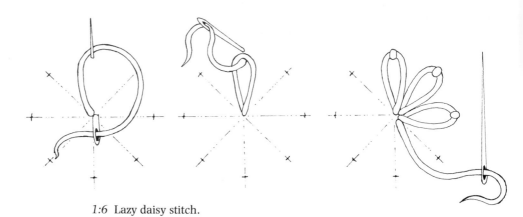

1:6 Lazy daisy stitch.

Star stitch
This is used to make a star shape, worked by crossing threads or by radiating threads from the centre (*1:7*).

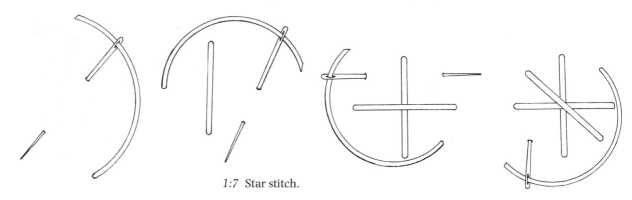

1:7 Star stitch.

Knots
Knots are common to European, Chinese, Japanese and Indian embroideries. They can be used as single motifs or massed together. To make a simple French knot, insert your needle into the fabric as in *1:8*. Wind the single thread round the needle according to the size of knot you want. Pull the needle through and secure the knot by pushing the needle back through the fabric (*1:9*).

1:8 French knots.

1:9 French knots.

Herringbone

Herringbone is a form of cross stitch. It can be used in a number of ways: on its own; as the foundation of interlacing stitch; or ornamented by couching its crosses. In Indian embroidery two rows of herringbone are worked, which intersect with each other to create a dense stitch which is often used for infilling.

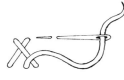

1:10 Herringbone stitch.

Herringbone is formed by crossing your thread from a bottom left point across to the top right, then to the top left and down to the right (*1:10*). The size of the stitch can be varied to give a more open or compacted stitch.

Cross stitch

Cross stitch is a universal stitch made up of two straight lines, singly, as a continuous row or randomly arranged. Illus. *1:11* shows a contemporary pictorial embroidery by Julia Pullen of her two daughters. The entire ground is covered with minute cross stitches.

To make regular cross stitches, draw crosses with a fabric pen or use a fabric weave where you can count the threads. Starting from underneath, bring the needle through bottom left to top right, then across to top left and finally back to bottom right. Or repeat the first diagonal along a row of cross stitches, and back along the row with the other diagonal.

1:11 Cross-stitch picture by Julia Pullen.

1:12 Cross stitch.

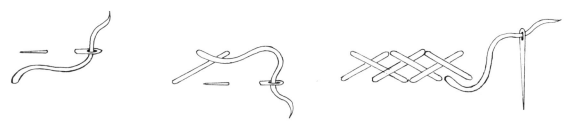

1:13 Elongated cross stitch.

1:14 Left: quilted cushion with mirror work by Amira Ahmed. *Right:* embroidered cushion with mirror work by Shahnaz Aslam.

1:15 Floral roundel by Poonam Peswani.

Projects

All the stitches we have looked at can be used to decorate all kinds of textiles. You could embroider a cushion (*1:14*) or a picture for your home; a badge for a blazer or a dress decoration; accessories – bag, belt, hat; fabric shoes and wall hangings. These are just a few suggestions.

The roundel (*1:15*) by Poonam Peswani makes an attractive picture, embroidered on cream silk with cotton in red and a variety of pastel colours. The floral motifs are mainly in compacted satin stitch with spiralling chain stitch and French knots forming the centres. Four carnations are worked in running stitch and the stems in stem stitch. The border is red silk decorated with machine embroidery in red scallop stitch and silver metal running stitch, edged with cream silk.

The Demon King by Amira Ahmed (*1:16*) is a humorous embroidered picture freely worked in random running stitches. Black stranded cotton is worked in a variety of thicknesses on a green silk ground. Similarly Amira has spontaneously stitched a personal badge (*1:17*). Two layers of peacock blue silk with wadding sandwiched between and a random running stitch in yellow stranded cotton have created a quilted effect. Such a badge can be sewn to any garment.

Embroidered furnishings can add richness to any living room. The cushions (*1:14*) are worked in machine and hand embroidery and mirror work on a gold yellow silk fabric. The left hand cushion has abstract floral motifs in red satin stitch with black embroidered mirror work centres surrounded with a machine embroidered red scallop stitch, edged with a red silk frill. The cushion on the right is machine quilted with abstract floral motifs in each corner and in the centre. The petals are worked in red satin stitch with black embroidered mirror work for the centres.

1:16 Embroidered picture of Ravana, the Demon King, by Amira Ahmed.

1:17 Quilted badge with initial by Amira Ahmed.

The Indian Sub-continent

Introduction

It is believed that most embroidery stitches can be found in India and Pakistan. Excavations have uncovered embroidery needles from between 2300 and 1500 B.C. and there has been a great wealth of embroideries handed down through the generations. Marco Polo observed as early as the twelfth century the exceptional beauty of Indian embroideries when he visited Gujurat. Unfortunately, many of the skills in design and execution are disappearing because of demands for cheaper textiles and of the pressures of Western culture. It is only in the more rural, tribal and isolated areas, such as Kutch in Gujurat, that these developments have not yet taken their toll.

The making of beautiful things is regarded as bringing good fortune and also plays an important role in social life. Embroidered fabrics are used in religious and marriage ceremonies; as an essential part of a girl's dowry; in rituals and festivals; for domestic furnishings and to caparison horses, camels, donkeys and bullocks. Traditionally girls begin to embroider their dowries at six years of age. As the women tend to spend most of their time in and around the home, much time is spent embroidering. The colours and patterns are often symbolic; for example, red is regarded as bringing good fortune and is therefore used for embroideries in a girl's dowry.

Many of the early embroideries we shall be looking at form part of a collection belonging to Moira Broadbent and are from nomadic or semi nomadic tribes of Sind, Rajasthan and Gujurat, with a few from Uzbek (a Soviet republic north of Afghanistan), many of which have been passed down through generations.

The designs are Muslim or Hindu, influenced by the many people who have invaded and since occupied these regions over the centuries. The most popular stitches are satin, herringbone, double ladder, chain, running and couching, often combined with mirror work. Some of these stitches have been illustrated on pages 14–17. Cotton, silk and wool fabric and threads are used. Floss silk thread is very popular for its shiny quality. Traditionally natural colours from plants were used but they have been largely replaced by synthetic dyes.

Plants and flowers

Plants and flowers have long provided food, medicine, cosmetics and dyes. They have also been considered to have a magic significance and many civilisations have invested particular flowers and herbs with forms of symbolism.

Animals

Animals, whether real or imaginary, have social and symbolic importance and are seen in many textiles.

The horse is the most important animal amongst Muslims. It is a symbol of social power and is often used in marriage, religious and military ceremonies. It also symbolises speed and pride. Muslim embroideries tend to be highly stylized and geometric as the Koran forbids the depiction of human and animal forms. In the case of animals, embroideries are often carried out *for* them.

Sind
Plate 2 shows a very finely embroidered horse chest band, mainly of geometric shapes in satin stitch. The borders are of minute cross stitches with cotton threads couched with herringbone stitch, embellished with mirrors arranged in diagonal patterns.

1:18 Horse chest band from Sind, Pakistan (Moira Broadbent).

1:19 Horse chest band (Moira Broadbent).

Illus. *1:18* and *1:19* also show horse chest bands from Sind with abstract floral motifs, a couched border embroidered in double ladder stitch with mirror work in maroon, deep red, yellow and cream. The bands are trimmed with maroon cotton tassels and beads of red and clear glass.

Illus. *1:19* is also worn by a horse as a head cover. This elaborate nomadic embroidery is from Sind, and of Muslim origin. The overall pattern is of abstract floral motifs based on trefoils (the main central floral shape of stitched double ladder stitch). The border shows trefoil and daisy shapes, with an edging of cotton tassels, glass beads and sequins.

Illus. *1:20* is another horse head dress of Muslim design, with an interesting pattern change in each section. The mainly geometric pattern is in satin stitch of stylized crosses, star and daisy shapes. The centres of the daisy shapes are in eyelet stitch. The head dress is stitched with floss silks of purple, orange and olive green with mirror work in deep red. The entire edge is embellished with transparent white, blue, red, orange and green glass beads. The strings shown at each end are used to tie the head dress onto the ears and muzzle of the horse.

1:20 Horse head dress from Sind, Pakistan (Moira Broadbent).

1:21 Tent hanging from Uzbek,
U.S.S.R. (Moira Broadbent).

Uzbek

Illus. *1:21* and *1:22* are nomadic embroideries from Uzbek. These Uzbek embroideries were embroidered by the women whilst the men did the heavy work, hunting and erecting the tents. Textiles such as carpets and animals (camels) were exchanged in the towns for food and raw materials (cotton, silks, beads and sequins). Embroideries from this region are similar to Persian designs, usually of stylized geometric or floral shapes in a single or repeat pattern. Illus. *1:21* is a tent hanging and may possibly have been used also for animal decoration. The stylized floral motifs are embroidered in silk floss using an interesting long twisted and couched stitch called Bokhara couching, traditionally used for filling in large floral motifs. This embroidery is in a variety of beautifully balanced colours, of apple green, antique white, marigold, cerise, royal blue and magenta. The border is in tiny cross and running stitches. Illus. *1:22* is believed to be a tent hanging. Cross stitches in magenta, yellow, black, pale blue-grey and dark green completely cover a canvas ground fabric, forming stylized medallion shapes which are probably of Persian influence. The embroidery is edged with magenta silk fabric and tassels with embroidered beads made with matching coloured silks.

Animals are greatly revered by the Hindus, regarded as sacred and traditionally were greatly adorned with elaborate embroideries covering their heads, backs and horns in the case of the bull.

The elephant is regarded as bringing good fortune, a symbol of wisdom and revered in the cast for its strength and stability. The elephant-headed god, Ganesh, is often petitioned for success before any enterprise, an important feature in Hindu worship and temple architecture.

Birds in Hindu mythology have important status. Represented in flight they are free spirits, therefore having an elusive character whereas when seen nestling in the trees they symbolise the souls of the faithful.

Peacocks and parrots are sacred birds mentioned in the *Rig Vedas*, the Hindu collection of sacred writings of A.D. 1200 The peacock symbolises several things. Represented on its own it symbolises the absent lover, hence its appearance on the bokano (*Plate 4*), and when presented as a pair denotes the poignancy of separated lovers. The peacock's cry is said to warn of rains and the bird can therefore symbolise the onset of the monsoons and the desire for rain by the nomads, as it does on the bullock cover (*Plate 3*).

Gujurat

The bullock cover (*Plate 3*) is from a semi nomadic tribe of Hindus from Gujurat in India who graze their cattle in Gujurat and neighbouring Rajasthan according to the dry and wet monsoon seasons. This pictorial cover uses a favourite stitch of this region, a compacted herringbone stitch of untwisted cotton on a cotton ground, used for infilling shapes. (This method of embroidering solid shapes probably preceded the use of appliqué, which was much quicker to do.) Favourite gods and sacred birds (peacocks and parrots and elephants) form the main part of the design, bordered with trefoils.

An interesting shaped embroidery is the bullock head dress from Gujurat (*Plate 4*) depicting abstract patterns, identified by their feet and claws. This forms part of a pair and was made by the Mochis, a sedentary tribe often referred to as the untouchables as they worked with skins and are famous for shoe making. This design is embroidered in cotton on a cotton ground. The stitch is tambour work, a type of chain stitch where a hook is used instead of a needle to make each stitch. This embroidery is decorated with glass bugle beads which glisten in the sunlight and jangle as the animal .noves. The centres of flowers are ornamented with mirrors.

Dress

The wearing of embroidered clothes still plays an important role in these countries, more commonly worn by women in the more rural areas. Often embroidery is executed on only parts of the garment such as collars, cuffs and yokes.

Sind

Plate 4 shows a bokano from a nomadic tribe in Sind, Pakistan. A bokano is a type of long scarf used for securing the purgaree or turban worn by a bridegroom when riding on horseback to his bride on his wedding day. The entire length would be wrapped round the turban and across the face hiding the groom's teeth and keeping the desert sand out of his face. It is regarded as a sign of bad luck if he reveals his teeth and naturally degrading if the bokano falls off. This particular embroidery is unusual because it is made up of two different patterns. These may have come from two different tribes and perhaps jointly symbolise the unification of the two families. Both patterns are worked in floss silk on a cotton ground. The end panels have a key-patterned border with floral motifs arranged in a square, embroidered in double ladder stitch. There is a stylized peacock surrounded by trefoils and seated on what is perhaps a stylized tree of life. The central panel is a very stylized geometric pattern in shaded satin stitch.

Uzbek

An attractive feature of men's costume in Uzbek is the wearing of hose tops traditionally worn by the nomadic or semi nomadic tribes. Illus. *1:23* is embroidered with silk on a cotton ground, embroidered with gold, yellow and purple chain stitch on a magenta silk. The central area is embroidered with a boteh motif – mango leaf originating in Persia. The hose is edged

1:22 Tent hanging from Uzbek, U.S.S.R. (Moira Broadbent).

1:23 Hose band (Moira Broadbent).

with a bilberry coloured silk. Illus. *1:24* is an extremely fine embroidery in counted canvas stitch following the warp and weft of the cloth and completely covering it. The motifs are heraldic, believed to be of Persian origin, embroidered in red, purple, green, maroon orange silk with the top half of the hose in red.

1:24 Hose band (Moira Broadbent).

Afghanistan

Embroidery has an important tradition in Afghanistan. In an area surrounded by Iran, Pakistan and the U.S.S.R. a blend of styles has naturally developed. Commonly used stitches are herringbone and chain with mirror work.

All the Afghan embroideries illustrated are the work of Aquela Feroz, a teacher from Kabul. Garments for men, women and children are embroidered using a variety of stitches.

1:25 Decorative yoke by Aquela Feroz.

Yokes form part of the women's traditional dress which is usually ankle length, worn with loose fitting trousers, drawn at the waist with cord. The yoke (*1:25*) is embroidered on a red cotton ground with green chain and stepped satin stitches (*1:26* and *1:27*). The star shaped motifs are predominantly of gold metal thread with some white stars along the edge.

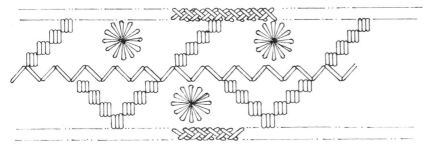

1:26 Dress: detail of front yoke panel.

1:27 Dress: detail of border motif.

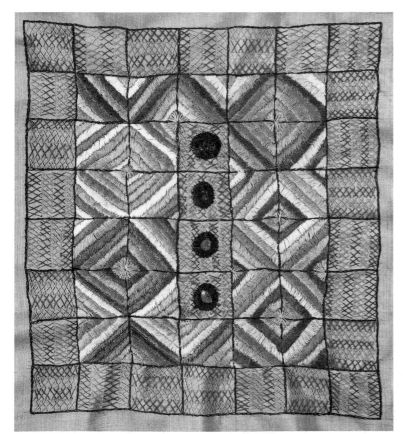

1:28 Afghan yoke with mirror work by Aquela Feroz.

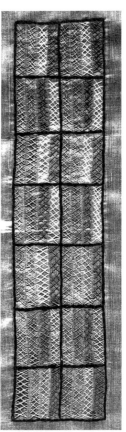

1:29 Embroidered cuff by Aquela Feroz to match the Afghan yoke.

The yoke (*1:28*) shows an unusual combination of brightly coloured embroidery in stranded cottons on a cerise silk ground. The overall geometric design is patterned with a purple and green herringbone border and uniformly divided into squares, outlined in black chain stitch. Dense satin stitch of randomly distributed colours of purple, blue, green, orange, yellow, cream and red occupy the main part of the yoke. The centre is embroidered in royal blue star stitches with mirror work. The matching cuffs are embroidered in green, orange, and yellow herringbone stitch; subdivided into rectangles which are outlined in black chain stitch.

Illus. *1:30* is an exquisitely embroidered dress in typical Kandahar design. The yoke is embroidered in maroon, orange, green and royal blue cotton thread in a close buttonhole stitch where no ground fabric is visible. The yoke border, cuffs and sleeves are embroidered in red herringbone stitch, forming lozenge shapes with green filling stitch and green cross stitches on the sleeves. The waist is patterned with green, red and peach chain stitch. The skirt has vertical patterns of red chain and feather stitches with the skirt border in green and orange cross stitches and green interlaced herringbone stitch, creating a trellis effect.

1:30 Afghan dress based on models from Kandahar, by Aquela Feroz.

For special occasions men wear embroidered garments and hats. Illus. *1:31* is a boy's shirt worn on special occasions such as weddings or going to the mosque. It is exquisitely embroidered all over the front panel with white silk threads on a white cotton ground. The embroidery is in geometric blocks of shaded satin stitch with random stylized floral motifs composed of rhombic shapes (*1:32* to *1:37*).

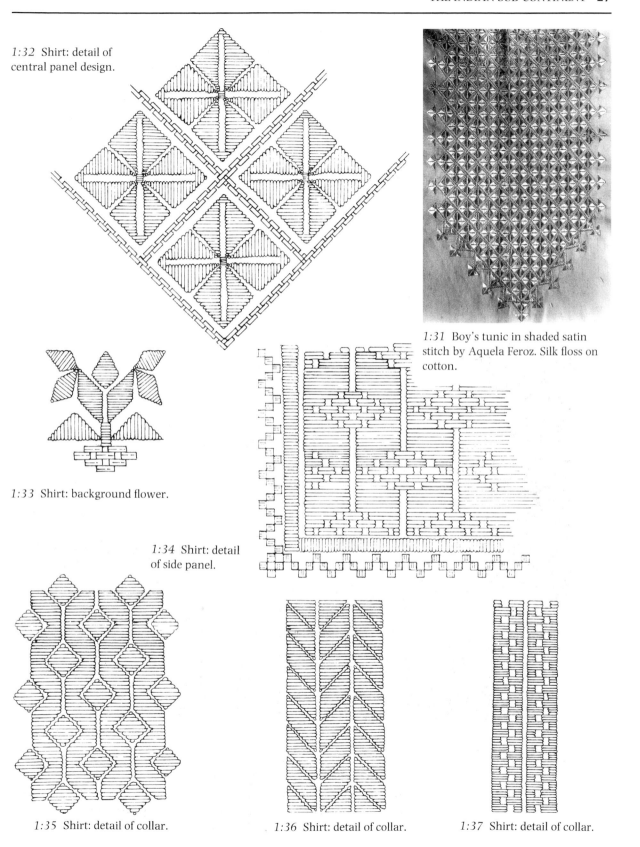

1:32 Shirt: detail of central panel design.

1:31 Boy's tunic in shaded satin stitch by Aquela Feroz. Silk floss on cotton.

1:33 Shirt: background flower.

1:34 Shirt: detail of side panel.

1:35 Shirt: detail of collar.

1:36 Shirt: detail of collar.

1:37 Shirt: detail of collar.

1:38 Afghan skull cap
by Aquela Feroz.

Skull caps are worn by men, and sometimes by women and boys. Afghan caps come in a variety of shapes, basically rounded, flat or pointed. Illus. *1:38* is flat topped, embroidered with stranded cottons on a turquoise silk ground. The pattern is executed in a continuous chain stitch with abstract leaf (Paisley) shapes in the centre with random French knots embroidered in peach, black, red, green, white and ochre colours.

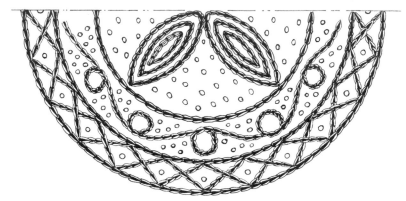

1:39 Cap: detail of crown design.

Mirror work

This is more correctly referred to as shisha mirror work, which is practised widely in India, Pakistan and Afghanistan. This is a style of embroidery that incorporates the use of pieces of mirror or mica in a variety of sizes, usually rounded in shape, to decorate embroideries combined with other stitches. Mica was traditionally used and is a mineral found as small glittering scales which can be separated into thin plates. The mirrors are secured to the ground fabric by embroidering a ring of stitches interlaced around a central loop which eventually encircles the piece of mirror (*1:51* and *1:55*). Designers in the West have incorporated mirrors in their designs, creating new ways of attaching mirrors to fabrics. Pockets made of transparent fabrics such as mesh, plastics and other materials are a few examples. The basic difference between the stitching of mirror work and that of other styles of embroidery is that it is worked in a circle and not in a straight line.

Traditional shisha work is used to ornament garments and other decorative items – animal regalia and soft furnishings of the peoples of Sind, Gujarat, Rajasthan, Baluchistan and Afghanistan. The mirrors are often used to emphasise the centres of flowers, the eyes of animals and birds.

Mirror work is most commonly practised in arid regions and is perhaps favoured for its shiny jewel-like quality which reflects the blue skies to give the illusion of water. It was also commonly believed that evil spirits would be warded off by seeing their own reflection in the mirrors.

In the villages outside Jaisalmer, a desert region in Rajasthan, mirrors are not only used to ornament garments but are also inset round the doorways of the traditional sandstone homes. The grand palaces of the

Maharajas in Udaipur and Jodphur and Amber fort are decorated, in particular on ceilings and walls, with mirrors that form an integral part of the architectural design. This gives the buildings a jewel like quality.

Illus. *1:40* is a modern example of shisha mirror work forming the yoke of a shalwar kameez. The mirror work is combined with stylized star motifs and random crosses, embroidered with purple stranded cotton on a lilac silk sateen ground to form a dense and highly textured pattern. It is still common to see parts of garments such as yokes, cuffs and collars embroidered with mirrors.

Illus. *1:41* shows a dress from Baluchistan. This is the typical style of dress called a kus which is worn with baggy trousers. This is a modern kus which does not have the richness of colour of a traditional kus, though the embroidery is still traditional. The cuffs, front and back and the large central pocket are embroidered on a cream silk with red and black stranded cotton. The red threads are couched with black, a traditional Baluchi style of embroidery. Stylized floral medallions with mirror centres ornament the front.

In Afghanistan, particularly in the region of Kandahar, shisha work is still widely used to decorate garments and the traditional Muslim skull cap. Illus. *1:28* and *1:29* show a modern yoke and matching cuffs, embroidered on silk in stranded cotton combined with mirror work.

1:40 Shalwar kameez yoke with mirror work by Amira Ahmed.

1:41 Modern kus with mirror work from Baluchistan, Pakistan (Tasneem Raja).

How to embroider with mirrors

The mirrors are available from specialist craft supermarkets and suppliers, and South Asian fabric shops. They are usually rounded and sold by the dozen and are relatively inexpensive. Occasionally they can be bought in a greater variety of shapes (lozenge, square or triangular) and colours.

Fabrics such as a strong silk, cotton or wool are best as the weight of the mirrors may distort your cloth otherwise. Choose a strong thread such as stranded cotton or silk to attach the mirrors.

The mirrors can be attached to your fabric at the start to form the basic pattern, while you stitch or when you have completed the embroidery. If you do the latter do remember to leave sufficient room to attach your mirrors.

Mirrors can be attached to your embroidery by one of two methods. The first explanation follows the traditional method and the second method is a much simplified version shown to me by one of my students.

Traditional mirror work

This method requires the forming of a grid over the mirror which will be interlaced with embroidery stitches worked to form a kind of open pocket for the mirror.

Secure the end of your thread with a knot. Hold the mirror firmly in place with your left thumb and make two vertical and parallel stitches following (*1:42* and *1:43*).

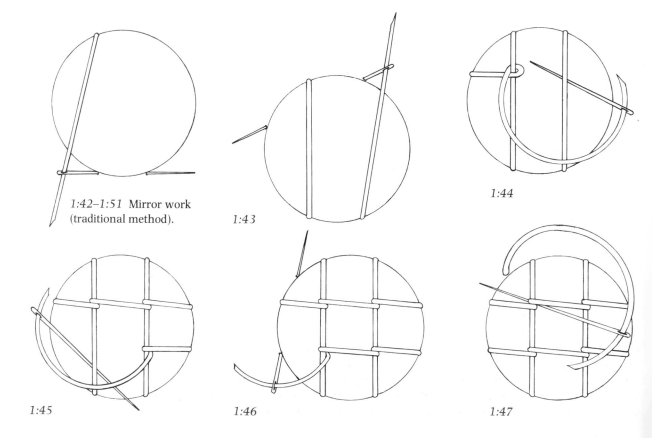

1:42–1:51 Mirror work (traditional method).

1:43

1:44

1:45

1:46

1:47

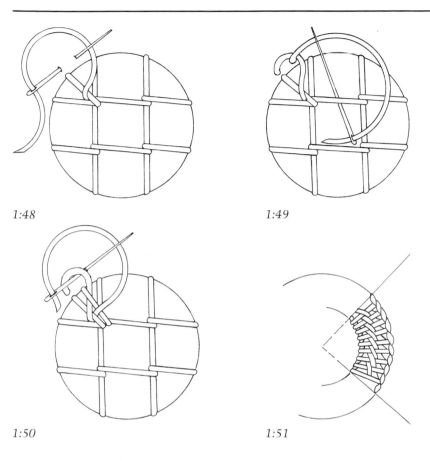

1:48

1:49

1:50

1:51

Work in stem stich from left to right and then right to left making sure you maintain the basic criss cross structure (1:44 and 1:45).

Turn the work round so that the stem stitches faces you vertically. This will make the work easier to handle. Slip your needle over and under the first bottom left hand interlacing. Pull the needle through and working in a clockwise direction make a small chain stitch at the outer edge of the mirror (1:48). Repeat this step in the same section (1:49 and 1:50) and continue round the mirror until the mirror is completely encircled with embroidery.

Variation of mirror work
This simply involves the making of an embroidered circle just slightly smaller then the mirror so as to cover it. This is then couched to the fabric with tiny stitches. Take a cylindrical object such as a pencil, piece of dowling or cane that is slightly smaller than the mirror piece you are going to use, or use a finger. Thread a needle and with your thread wind it around your object to the desired thickness and tie around a pencil. The thicker the thread the thicker the mirror work. Hold in place and slip the needle under the threads passing needle through loop to make a blanket stitch (1:52).

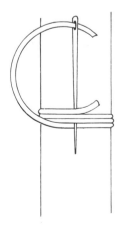

1:52–1:55 Mirror work (simplified method).

Repeat this continuing clock wise (*1:53* and *1:54*). The closer the stitch the firmer the circle.

Place the completed circle over the mirror securing with your left thumb. With a fine thread and needle make tiny stitches catching the edge of the embroidered circle and attach it to the fabric (*1:55*).

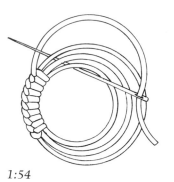

1:53

1:54

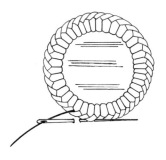

1:55 ·

Plate 1 Horse head dress from Sind, Pakistan (Moira Broadbent).

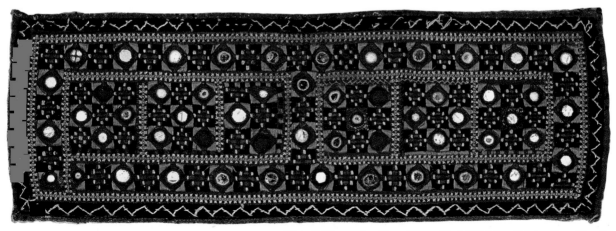

Plate 2 Horse chest band from Sind, Pakistan (Moira Broadbent).

Plate 3 Embroidered bullock cover from Gujurat, India (Moira Broadbent).

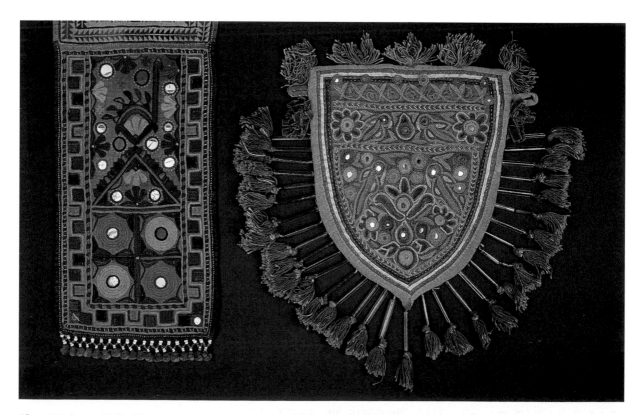

Plate 4 Bokano (for holding turban) from Sind, Pakistan. Bullock head dress
from Gujurat, India (Moira Broadbent)

2 Appliqué

Introduction

Appliqué is the name given to the technique of stitching pieces (usually shaped pieces) of fabric to a fabric background. The pieces can be of woven fabrics such as cotton, silk, linen and wool, and non wovens which include animal skins and fur pelts, leather and felt. There can be further embellishment with decorative embroidery stitches, trimmings, beads, shells and sequins.

Most cultures use appliqué for both decorative and more utilitarian purposes such as the strengthening of materials. Many of you have probably at some time patched up holes in clothes, in particular at the knees and elbows where wear and tear are at their greatest, by laying a piece of fabric over the hole.

Appliqué can also be used to make thick, warm and waterproof fabrics which can be easily inlaid and padded to create warm and hard wearing fabrics. Appliqué is, therefore, the most commonly used form of embroidery amongst the peoples of cooler regions: the Inuit Indians of Greenland, the Laps of Northern Scandinavia and the peoples of the mountainous regions of Central Asia. Here such local materials as the fur and skin of caribou, reindeer and seals, fish skins and wool are used. However, nowadays clothes are mostly imported and industrially produced. The latest wind and waterproof materials tend to be lighter and less bulky than traditional clothing.

Felt appliqué is one of the oldest forms of appliqué. It used to be widely practised by nomadic cattle breeding tribes who wandered between the Russian Balkans and the Gobi Desert as far back as 200 B.C. Saddle covers and a wall hanging (possibly earlier) have been found in Siberian tombs. The latter shows rows of figures and bands of floral patterns.

Some of the earliest examples of appliqué are overlaid appliqué such as the woven roundels, squares, strips and L-shaped corner pieces that were stitched onto plain linen robes by the Copts of Egypt between A.D. 300 and 1000. Tapestries with images of beautifully observed plants, animals, birds, portraits and dancing figures in splendid decorative patterns were found in Egyptian burial sites.

During the Middle Ages of Europe, inlaid appliqué was used as a cheaper substitute for embroidery. Specific shapes were set into corresponding shapes in a ground fabric. The raw edges were sewn together and hidden by embroidery stitches or couched work, this adding an attractive decorative edge to the appliqué piece.

This technique was employed for heraldic banners at secular ceremonies, pageants and festivals, for altar fronts and vestments, and for chair and horse furniture. The use of solid bright colours and bold motifs made eye-catching displays.

Among the early European settlers of North America were the Pennsylvanian Dutch who arrived in the seventeenth and eighteenth centuries. The inclement weather and lack of materials encouraged the recycling of old clothes and quilts, used in new designs. As a result, there grew a tradition and the widespread use of appliqué and patchwork quilts. Appliqué was also used to decorate aprons. The designs were usually symmetrical and often showed tulips, hearts and birds.

Appliqué has been widely practised in India for centuries. A particular craft in the eighteenth and nineteenth centuries was that of leather appliqué. The Mochis of Kutch, part of Gujurat, learnt their skills from Muslim craftsmen at the end of the sixteenth or beginning of the seventeenth century. Black, red and green leather were used for the purpose, and embroidered with chain stitch of silver and gold. Leather appliqué was also used to cover shields in Kutch and in nearby Sind (in Pakistan). These shields were then tooled and painted, and armoured with metal bosses.

European missionaries to Hawaii in the nineteenth century introduced skills of appliqué and quilting which became combined with native designs inspired by indigenous fruits (such as the pineapple and breadfruit) arranged asymmetrically. The designs were cut directly from folded fabric which repeated the motif many times. Usually two or three colours occupy a printed calico ground. Few crafts people practise the skills today so the tradition is disappearing.

Fashionable in the nineteenth century was the importing into Europe of patterned textile chintz from India. These fabrics, usually showing birds and foliage, were cut up and stitched to plain grounds to make such items as quilts. Although very much like overlaid appliqué, this method is also known as cretonne appliqué or broderie perse.

The second half of this century has seen the evolution of protest art, in response to the historical, social, political and economic changes this century, in the form of paintings, drawings, sculpture and textiles. People throughout the world both directly or indirectly have portrayed their experiences visually. Strong images of repression and oppression with often symbolic meanings can be seen in the appliqués of the Chilean women who have lived under a military dictatorship since 1973; the CND banners protesting against nuclear war and power; the Greenham Common Womens banners protesting against the siting of cruise missiles since 1981; the Anti Apartheid movement protesting against the injustices of the present South African régime.

Modern day fashion designers often incorporate appliqué for both fashion garments and for advertising a particular brand of sportswear and accessories in the form of industrially produced appliquéed logos. These logos have become status symbols. Contemporary textile artists too have explored appliqué, creating exciting wall hangings, soft furnishings and garments exhibited in galleries, incorporated in Interior design and Public buildings.

Shadow work is another style of appliqué where shapes are cut from fabric and stitched behind a transparent fabric such as fine silk, cotton or muslin, creating a shadow effect through the materials. With the availability of many varieties of natural and synthetic materials – plastics, mesh, etc, many artists have explored shadow work to create exciting two and three dimensional textiles.

Another important appliqué technique is reverse appliqué. This method involves the cutting away of shapes and layers of material to reveal the different coloured layers, the opposite of most other appliqué techniques. This has been used by the Cuna Indians with unique vitality, which shall be dealt with later.

Hand appliqué

Hand appliqué is a method of applying one fabric to another by stitching by hand round the edge, it is the method used for both the *Bowl of Apples* wall hanging and the bag and belt. In this method you need to mark the shape on the back of the fabric motif that is to be applied (*2:1*) and then fold in the 1 cm turning that you will need (*2:2* and *2:3*). The edges of the lozenge shape (used for the belt featured on page 50) where they curve need to be clipped to the shape of the motif, then turned under, tack the shape, then pin on the background fabric and tack into place then slip-stitch around the edge.

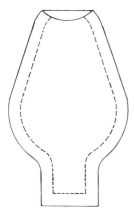

2:1 Tree shape.

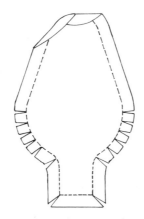

2:2 Clip and turn in edge.

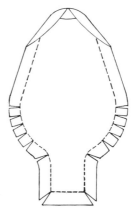

2:3 Clip and turn in edge.

To emphasize the shape of the motif (*2:7* to *2:10*) show how you can use decorative stitches round the edges of the shapes that have been appliquéed.

The design can be from imagination or from a photograph or a postcard (for enlarging a picture see page 122). Bear in mind when choosing a suitable picture that it should be fairly simple, for you can always add interest by using embroidery stitches to enhance the design and give it more colour and texture. Do not try to make too complicated a design by hand appliqué because unless you are using non frayable materials such as felt, leather or suede, edges have to be turned under before they are stitched to the background and this is difficult with very elaborate shapes.

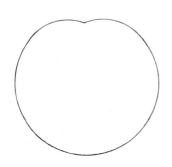

2:4 Apple template.

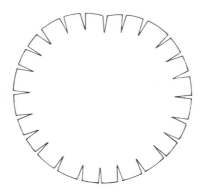

2:5 Apple shape cut out in fabric and clipped.

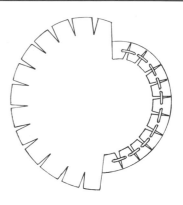

2:6 Turn in clipped edge and tack.

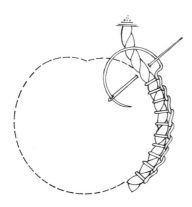

2:7 Attach cord to edge with blanket stitch.

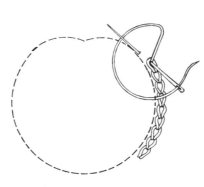

2:8 Chain stitch.

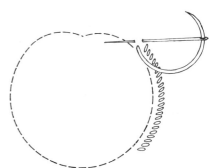

2:9 Stem stitch.

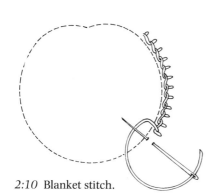

2:10 Blanket stitch.

Illus. *2:11*. Draw out the design to scale on a piece of paper, then trace off each part of the design onto tracing paper. Indicate on the original design the colours to be used and give each section of the design a number and put the same number on the same area of the tracing (*2:13*). If you do not number the pieces if can be confusing to assemble all the pieces as they are a bit like a jigsaw puzzle.

You can use the tracing to make stout paper templates for the shapes to be appliquéed (*2:14*). Cut out the templates and pin onto the appropriate fabric using the lengthwise or crosswise grain only. Mark the actual shapes of the pieces round the edges with fabric marker pen or lightly with pencil. Then add 1 cm seam allowance all round the edges. Cut out each piece with sharp scissors, working carefully round the marked shape. In order to be able to turn the seam allowance under curved edges and to keep it flat, snip from the raw edge to the marked shape as often as necessary.

Turn the edges in to the wrong side carefully ensuring that the shape you make is smooth with no awkward points sticking out. As you turn the edge in you can tack it down into place with a contrasting thread. When you have tacked all the pieces it is time to assemble them onto the background.

Bowl of apples wall hanging

The background is a white square of cotton fabric measuring 80×80 cm, the appliqué shapes of cotton, polyester cotton and felt.

Start by pinning 5 mauve pieces onto the white background to form the diagonal stripes. The pieces on the outside can be left with their raw edges open as these will be sewn under the border stripes. Tack into place and then slipstitch onto background with colour matching thread, making the stitches as small as possible. Sew all the stripes on in the same way and then take the bowl shape and choose its position on top of the stripes. Take the apples one by one and arrange them in their appropriate position. When you are pleased with the arrangement, sew the apples on first and then sew the bowl on, so that it overlaps the apples.

Cut shapes from white felt for the highlights on the apples and grey felt for the stalks. These felt shapes can be stitched straight back on the background fabric as they have no fraying edges to be turned under.

Cut 4 strips of fabric 70 cm long to make the inner border. Tack them into position and make sure at this stage that the picture is really square by checking that all the sides are the same. Sew on by machine. You can either finish off the ends square or you can mitre them by sewing them together diagonally at the ends, right sides together.

The final border strips measure 80×7 cm. Cut four strips of this size and tack then machine sew onto the inner border. In this wall hanging the corners are mitred. The wall hanging can be finished by turning in the edges with a 1.5 cm seam allowance or a good method is to use 2.5 cm wide bias binding which is sewn round the edge and turned under and slipstitched to the back.

2:12 Apple-shaped piece of fabric.

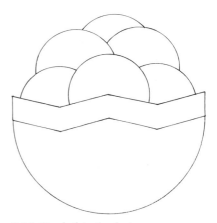

2:13 Bowl of Apples design.

2:11 Bowl of Apples appliqué wall hanging by Margo Singer.

2:14 Bowl of Apples templates.

Machine appliqué

Appliqué by machine is obviously faster and generally stronger than hand appliqué and can normally be done on most materials with the exception of the very heavyweight materials which cannot be fed through a machine. The advantage of machine appliqué is that there is no need to make turnings if you have a swing needle sewing machine – you can use a zigzag or close satin stitch round the edges, or you can sew with a straight stitch first and then couch down a thick thread which covers the raw edges and also enhances the shape of the design.

If the fabric to be applied to the background is at all lightweight or at all stretchy, it is a good idea to back the fabric with a lightweight iron-on Vilene. (This can be bought by the metre.) It is best to cut the Vilene a little bigger than the appliqué shape, and to iron it onto the back of the shape before trimming to size.

Illus. *2:15* shows a batik jacket. The triangular pieces of crackled fabric have been backed with Vilene and attached to the brown silk of the pieces of jacket with a normal straight machine stitch, approximately 3 mm from the edge of the appliqué shapes. They are then zigzagged onto the background using a satin stitch with the stitch width dial of the sewing machine set at 3. The satin stitch must be wide enough to cover the straight machine stitch and also extend far enough onto the background fabric to anchor the applied piece firmly.

2:15 Jap silk jacket by Margo Singer.

If you have intricate shapes to appliqué, an alternative to Vilene is Bondaweb which is a sticky film protected by backing paper. This can be ironed onto the fabric through the backing paper. The backing can then be peeled off. This is particularly good for very flimsy lightweight fabrics such as muslin and silk which fray easily. The Bondaweb can be applied before the appliqué shapes are cut out.

Reverse appliqué shapes

The name is given to a technique where shapes are cut out of layers of fabric instead of being built up. An exciting use of this technique has historically been found in mola work where a type of reverse appliqué is employed – layers are cut away as well as built up.

As a simple exercise, try two layers of contrasting fabric with a simple geometric or circular shape as in (*2:16* to *2:19*). Draw a shape onto fabric using a template made from card. The shapes illustrated can be used as single motifs, in repeat or combined together to make attractive designs. Place the template on the fabric and draw round. Follow instructions for the hat project pp. 45 to 49. Note in *2:16* to *2:19* where to clip fabric.

Many modern artists have explored reverse appliqué. Beatrice Williams has been making wall hangings for interiors. The hanging illustrated in *2:20* explores the use of overlaid and reverse appliqué to create this bold and tactile wall hanging, evocative of her interest in Asian dress and jewellery, and her interest in the folk arts. The pattern is based on units of stripes and illustrates an intuitive response to the use of materials and colour where a combination of applied layers of stitched and cut muslin and strips of fabric couched with machine zigzag stitch create an overall abstract design.

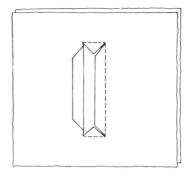

2:16 Oblong.

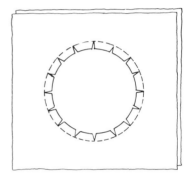

2:17 Circle.

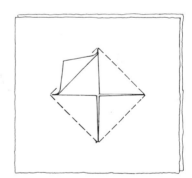

2:18 Square.

2:20 Appliqué wall hanging by Beatrice Williams. In a range of pastel-coloured fabrics, strips of leather and embroidery threads, from yellow ochre to lilac pink.

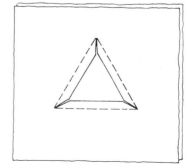

2:19 Triangle.

Reverse appliqué has also been used by artists to create interesting patterns on garments. Illus. *2:21* an attractive jacket made by Sarah Satchell. The entire jacket is made of reverse appliqué in layers of hand dyed muslin, with a zigzag machined stitched checkered design. Layers of muslin have been cut away at random to expose the different layers of colour. The colours have been inspired by Sarah's interest in medieval tiles – earthy antique sepia, green, red, blue, cream, ochre and orange.

2:21 Reverse appliqué jacket by Sarah Satchell.

World survey

Chile

The Chilean appliqués featured in *Plate 6* may appear 'naive' but they are making a powerful statement in a coded form to avoid censorship. They reflect the lives of the people living in the shanty towns of Santiago where poverty and unemployment are high and where there are shortages of food, clothing and basic amenities such as electricity, gas and water.

These subjects feature prominently in the composition of the appliqués. *Plate 6* illustrates women fetching water from a communal tap. Electricity is often obtained illegally from overhead cables. The backdrop of the appliqué, and to many appliqués, shows the Andes, which convey a sense of space in direct contrast to the overcrowded living conditions of the shanty towns. The women who make these appliqués are meeting socially as well as creating the appliqués which bring a small but important income through their sales internationally. The appliqués depict recurring situations such as reunions with lost relatives, searching for loved ones, cuts in an already inadequate health service, demands for justice, hopes for solidarity and unity of the world, celebrations and International Children's Day. The appliqués illustrate the strength and resilience of the human spirit for they combine the beauty of trees, plants and family life with the inhuman living conditions. And all the scenes are depicted in optimistic, brightly coloured cottons and threads.

Egypt

Animals were revered during the time of the Pharaohs and they were mummified and buried in the royal tombs. Many of the animals have been discovered wrapped in decorative appliqués. Excavations of Tutan-khamun's tomb revealed a collar made of linen, with petals in appliqué. This dates back 3000 years.

Other appliqués illustrated the world of the ancient Egyptians, by show-ing scenes from daily life. The tradition of appliqué persisted and centuries later they stylized geometric patterns typical of Muslim Art were used in tentmaking. Tentwork has now become synonymous with appliqué. Men can be found making appliqués, seated in small boothes on the street of the 'Tent Makers' in Old Cairo city at Bab Zuweyla. Traditionally these appliqués were used for special occasions. They were made into large ceremonial tents for use during religious festivals and funerals; they formed decortive borders for speakers' tables at public meetings, tempor-ary kiosks for the sale of confectionary during feast days and weekend meat days; and they served as striking awnings at the openings of new official public buildings.

Nowadays these appliqués are largely aimed at the tourist market and consequently have become cruder, with the appliqué often replaced by printed cloth, that gives the appearance of appliqué.

Northern climes

Traditionally the Inuit Indians made appliqué clothing with seal skins, embellished with beads, buttons, braids and bindings of seal's intestine and animal hair. Nowadays the creation of pictorial wall hangings has replaced the making of clothing. The hangings are made for sale. They illustrate the daily activities such as hunting and cleaning fish, and incor-porate animal and bird motifs that are important in Inuit Indian culture.

The Laps stripped seal pelts and decorated them for ceremonial clothing as they believed that seals have a special kinship with mankind. Woollen materials were made into clothing and wall hangings for the interiors of tents. Also woven braids and bands were applied to the traditional cos-tume which is only occasionally worn.

Amongst the North American Indians totem motifs (writings in pictor-ial code) recording gods in tribal history were used in body painting. These motifs were later adapted and applied to woven fabrics. Such applied fabrics were strong and hardy, worked by the women. Any spare materials were used to make mocassins, pouches, fringing and lacing which were often decorated with beads and shells.

India and Pakistan

Appliqués used to be made by the poorer farming people as they were quicker and cheaper to make than embroideries. The bold designs were often patchworks of fabric from old garments. However, increasingly printed imitation cloths are being used. Special appliqués were tra-ditionally used to decorate large festivals, for example religious days and weddings. Even today it is common to see weddings held under an appliquéd tent in a courtyard or open space.

Animals are greatly revered in India. Traditionally man has identified his strengths and weaknesses in them. He sees himself as having an animal and spiritual nature. Consequently animals such as the camel, bullock and horse were traditionally well decorated. The horns or heads were elaborately decorated with appliqués but also embroideries of shisha mirror work (see chapter 1). Appliqués were also traditionally used for animal harness as padded back clothes for draught animals where wear and tear is considerable. The bullock cover (2:22) is from a farming community of the Sind Thar border. This heraldic looking appliqué is made up of layers of brightly coloured cottons where red and blue dominate on a white cotton ground with a bold design of appliquéed shapes of interlacing scrolls and repeating geometric designs and abstracted floral motifs.

The bullock covers are usually made in pairs as draught animals are usually harnessed together. The hump of the cover would often be decorated with a stuffed bird, usually a sparrow perched on a hump.

2:22 Bullock cover from Gujurat, India (Moira Broadbent).

Iran

The region of Resht in Iran was famous for its particular style of inlaid appliqué. Images of flora and portraits of royalty were commonly worked as wall hangings using pieces of felt, woven wool or cotton applied to or inlaid to a ground of one of these materials, with the applied motifs held in place with tambour work. Often the wall hangings were embellished with tiny seed pearls, gold and silver thread couched with silk.

Thailand

In the northern hills of Thailand the Lisu and Meo people use a combination of appliqué and cross stitch in the decoration of the costumes used as daily wear and for special ceremonies. These costumes of blouses, skirts and aprons are usually dyed indigo with secular motifs of geometric patterns appliquéed in red, yellow and black, decorating the borders and panels of garments. These appliquéed patterns are often decorated with laid and couched work. In contrast the appliqués of the capital city of Bangkok to the south of Thailand tend to depict bold motifs of dragons and lions edged in chain and running stitch, and button embroidery.

Tibet

In Tibet appliqués made of silk, wool and cotton were traditionally used as wall hangings, tent panels, clothing and saddle covers. Images of mythological creatures such as dragons were depicted. The dragon is believed to have a vigilant character. Buddhist temples were decorated with appliquéed hangings known as tankas, usually with a central figure of a god or saint.

West Africa

Traditional appliqué in West Africa was worked by specially established family guilds. They worked personal designs, which were often heraldic, for civil and military ceremonies and for the ornament of clothes. This particular use of appliqué gave chiefs status and power. The Fon men of Dahomey produce woven cotton cloth which is used for striking appliqués of bird, animal, fish and fruit motifs, traditionally these related to kings. Battle scenes and ritual sacrifices are also commonly depicted. Nowadays these appliqués are generally used as wall hangings.

Mola work

The art of Mola work (Mola literally means blouse) is unique to Panama, in particular the San Blas Islands. During the seventeenth and eighteenth centuries the Cuna Indians fled to San Blas from mainland Panama because of Spanish invasion and led a closed tribal way of life preventing any foreign intrusion.

Traditionally the peoples of Panama wore body paint which depicted elaborate birds, beasts and trees in rich natural colours of red, yellow and blue. This was important to Cuna culture as it was a commonly held belief that it warded off the spirits.

Mola making is thought to have developed recently from the purchase of manufactured cloth and appliquéed hems from Europe, established through trading links in the nineteenth century and exchanged for islands products. In the mid nineteenth century the French Huguenots settled in Panama which encouraged the wearing of clothing and introduced embroidery skills. All these factors may have encouraged the use of fabrics and the evolution of mola making.

The only remaining sign of body painting is a single blue black line or abstract marking on the nose which is regarded as a sign of beauty. Molas are made up of two or more layers of cloth. The colours used are often akin to the colours traditionally used in body painting. Traditionally the colour and decoration of molas denoted rank and position in a tribe, worn at festivals and ceremonies.

No two molas are ever the same. There is an endless variety of plain and patterned sleeves, yokes and borders, often edged with rick-rack braiding and ruffles (*Plates 8 and 9*). New designs are usually made in secret for special occasions such as ceremonies and going to market. They are highly prized and only displayed on completion. The new mola is often concealed under an old one until the wearer arrives at her destination. Then the design is quickly memorised and reproduced by other Cuna women throughout the San Blas Islands.

Mola work is traditionally made by the Cuna women. However nowadays hand sewing machines are used to make up the blouses and machines are strictly the domain of men.

Traditionally images of flora, fauna, marine life (*2:23*), dreams and animal spirits are constant sources of inspiration for the Cuna people, which are represented in a stylized form on the blouses. Also geometric designs inspired by early wood carvings such as the zigzag saw tooth

2.23 Crab design in mola work (Liz Nuñez-Perez).

design which symbolises fertility and the umbilical cord and which is used in all the molas illustrated. The blouse design (*Plate 8*) is of the great turtle demon Miomuneki who is believed to obstruct the delivery of a child. *Plate 10* represents sea life possibly squid in an abstract way with random circles enclosing bird motifs. The influences of present day media, for example, posters, newspapers, advertising and radio have resulted in images of space ships, aeroplanes, submarines, political cartoons and advertisements of Coca Cola, etc, being used as mola designs. The influx of missionaries and the American Peace Corps have also had a profound influence on mola designs with Biblical stories appearing in mola designs.

Commercial pressures and tourism are slowly eroding the delicate balance of the traditional Cuna life. Nowadays many crude molas are being produced with simple designs and minimal skills for tourists and for American and European markets. However, the Cuna women wisely still keep the best molas for their families.

Mola technique

Molas are brightly coloured reverse appliqués, made up of two or more layers of fabric which are cut through to reveal layers of different colours, in a contour effect. Plain strong, closely woven cottons of contrasting colours are the most commonly used fabrics; patterned fabrics are often used for filling in small details and for making the borders and yokes.

Embroidery stitches such as cross, chain and running are used to outline and detail shapes.

Traditionally a deep red fabric was used for the main colour. However nowadays many bright colours are available and are in favour. The Cunas of Mamitupu have recently started making toy animals for foreign markets using a simplified version of traditional mola making (*Plate 11*). These make humourous and enchanting gifts.

Mola technique can be applied to clothing, fashion accessories (such as bags and hats) and soft furnishings (such as cushions and wall hangings).

2:24 Appliqué bag and belt with mola work hat.

Project – mola work hat

The hat is a three layered mola. As you become more skilled you can apply more layers.

Materials

Three pieces of cotton fabric, approx 35 cm for each, of turquoise, yellow and fuchsia red. To dye your own colours see page 56. When selecting your colours choose contrasting colours as this will create a more three dimensional effect in your mola. It is advisable to have a dark colour for the top layer to maximise this effect.

60 cm piping cord, (or measure according to size of crown)	Tape measure
1 m bias binding	Tailor's chalk
Machine thread	Compasses
Tacking thread	Dressmaker's or ordinary plain paper
Pins	Dressmaker's carbon
Sewing and embroidery needles	Fabric pen
Embroidery and dressmaking scissors	Tracing wheel

Method

Arrange colours as follows: turquoise first, then yellow and the top layer fuchsia red.

1   To make the Mola panel firstly cut your fabric into strips of 20 × 65 cm.

2   Line up fabrics carefully using pins to secure fabric in place.

3   Tack through all the layers of fabric as this will provide you with a more stable ground on which to draw your pattern.

4   To transfer the bird motif onto the fabric. Trace shape onto greaseproof, tissue or tracing paper. Enlarge according to the size your require. Enlarging any image can be achieved by scaling up on graph paper or by photocopying.

5   Draw the bird motif by drawing straight onto your fabric with a fabric pen (of which the ink is water soluble). Alternatively, sandwich a piece of dressmaker's carbon between the scale-up paper design and the top layer of fabric; draw round the design with a hard pencil or a tracing wheel.

6   Repeat the bird motif on the panel several times to fit the required crown size.

7   Use short tacking stitches to outline the design on the fabric following the line marked (*2:25* and *2:26*).

2:25 Bird motifs drawn with running stitch.

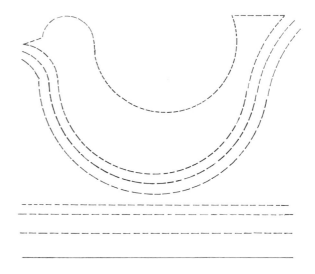

2:26 Sew lines of motif with tacking stitch. Top layer of fabric is marked 1.

8   With a pair of pointed embroidery scissors make a short cut of approximately 1.5 cm along the line marked (*2:27* and *2:28*) cutting through the top layer of fabric (red). Be very careful not to cut through the next layer (yellow).

9   Select a colour thread which matches the top layer and thread up an embroidery needle with the thread either single or double. Knot the end.

10   Use slipstitch to turn under the edges of background fabric (*2:28*). As you move round the outline, continue to cut and stitch a short

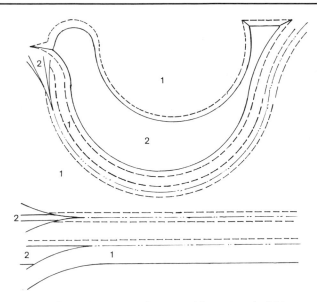

2:27 Cut where indicated to expose the second layer (marked 2).

2:28 Top layer cut and stitched back to reveal second colour.

distance at a time. Clip curves and corners where necessary. Always work from the centre outwards as this will keep your work flat.

11 When you have completed the first layer, remove the red fabric pieces of the bird. The yellow layer is now visible (*2:29*).

12 Repeat stages 1–11 to complete the nest layer, cutting through the second layer.

13 The turquoise layer is now visible (*2:30* and *2:31*). Press Mola panel with a warm iron. You may want to add some detail, such as eyes (*2:31*). Simply follow *2:17* to make a round shape. Slip a small piece of black fabric in between the first and second layer, using a small pair of pointed scissors to push the fabric into the opening you have just made. Slip stitch as before.

2:29 Second layer cut and stitched back to reveal third colour.

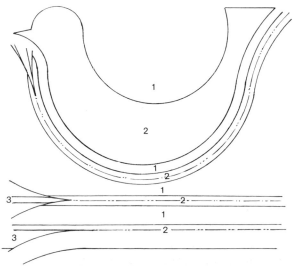

2:30 Continue.

2:31 Third colour revealed, with eye added for detail (optional).

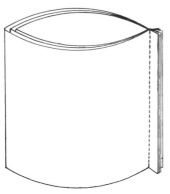

2:32 To make the main part of the hat, stitch panels with right sides together.

How to make up the mola hat

1 Fold mola panel with the front facing each other and the design matching exactly at the side. Pin, tack and machine in place (*2:32*).

2 Trim seam to 1 cm and bind this raw edge with bias binding.

3 To make this bias binding fold a length of approximately 15 cm. This can be done easily with a warm iron (*2:33*). Attach half the length of the bias binding to one side of the raw edge and the remainder over the other side (*2:34*). Machine in place.

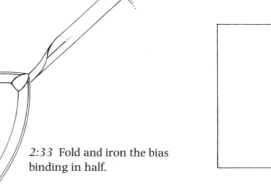

2:33 Fold and iron the bias binding in half.

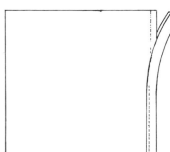

2:34 Use bias binding to cover the seam.

4 To make the top of the hat you need to make a template. Adjust according to particular crown size. Draw a circle with a radius of, say, 8 cm on a sheet of paper. Cut the circle out.

5 Pin the template to the fabric of the same colour as the top layer of the mola panel (red in this example). Cut two layers of fabric as this will give the hat top more body.

6 Draw round the template with tailor's chalk or a fabric pen. Cut fabric out (*2:35*).

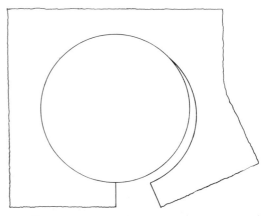

2:35 Cut out crown of hat.

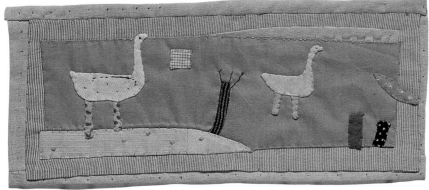

Plate 5 Appliqué pictures by Janet Bolton. They have a delightful naive quality which reflects a deep interest in folk arts. Simple shapes are patterned with printed cottons, sometimes embellished with beads and buttons.

Plate 6 Protest pictures, 'Don't cut off our water' and 'International Day of Children', from Chile (Chile Solidarity Campaign).

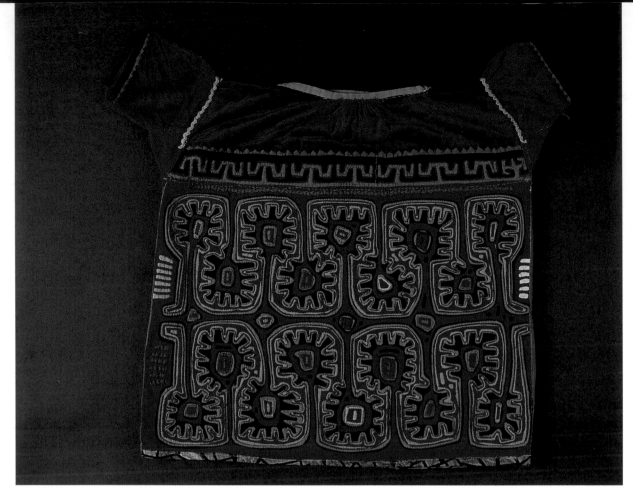

Plate 7 Early mola blouse from the island of Mamitupu, San Blas, Panama (Liz Nuñez-Perez).

Plate 8 Early 20th century mola blouse, with turtle design, from Chucunaque India, San Blas, Panama (Lady Richmond Brown Collection).

Plate 9 Contemporary mola work from the island of Mamitupu, San Blas, Panama. Cuna women wearing molas on the island of Mamitupu (Liz Nuñez-Perez).

Plate 10 Marine life and birds depicted in mola work, by Chucunaque Indians, San Blas, Panama (Lady Richmond Brown Collection).

Plate 11 Toy animals made from mola work, from the island of Mamitupu, San Blas, Panama (Liz Nuñez-Perez).

7 Keep the two layers together. Pin, tack and machine approximately 1 cm from the edge.

8 Piping is used to trim the edge of the hat top. To make the piping use either bias binding or choose a colour which matches the third layer, or a colour of your choice, (see instructions on page 108).

9 Attach the piping to the hat top (2:36), stitching and clipping the curved edge as you machine round (2:37).

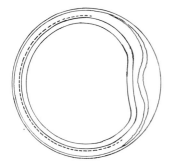

2:36 Stitch piping to edge of crown.   2:37 Piping in place.

10 Pin base of hat to the piped top with the front facing inwards (2:38). Match edges carefully in order to maintain the round shape of the hat. Tack in place. If you have a toque shaped hat makers stand use this to work on the hat. This will make the hatmaking process much easier.

11 Machine close to piping stitch.

12 Trim and clip this raw edge (2:39).

13 Bias bind circular edge (2:35, see instructions on page 108).

14 Hem the hat by first making a small turning of 3 mm to hide the raw edge then fold again 2 cm and hem with slipstitch (2:40).

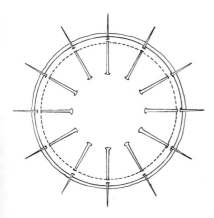

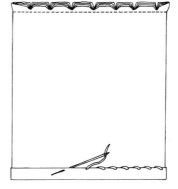

2:39 Stitch and clip.   2:40 Hem bottom edge of hat.

2:38 Pin crown to main part of hat.

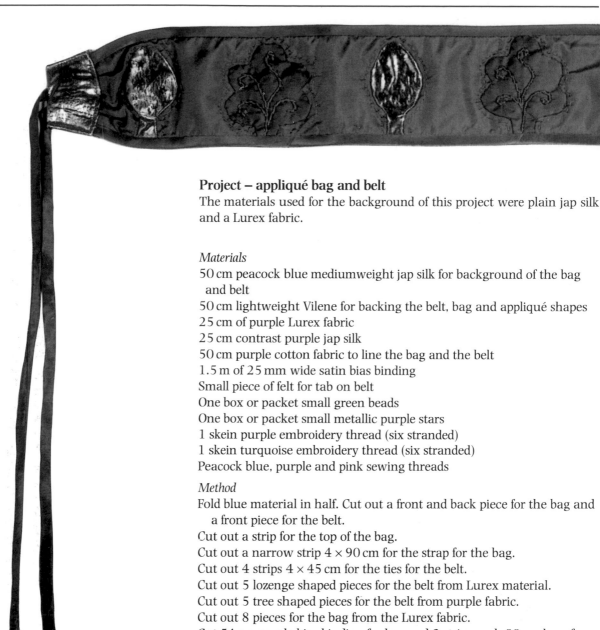

Project – appliqué bag and belt

The materials used for the background of this project were plain jap silk and a Lurex fabric.

Materials

50 cm peacock blue mediumweight jap silk for background of the bag and belt
50 cm lightweight Vilene for backing the belt, bag and appliqué shapes
25 cm of purple Lurex fabric
25 cm contrast purple jap silk
50 cm purple cotton fabric to line the bag and the belt
1.5 m of 25 mm wide satin bias binding
Small piece of felt for tab on belt
One box or packet small green beads
One box or packet small metallic purple stars
1 skein purple embroidery thread (six stranded)
1 skein turquoise embroidery thread (six stranded)
Peacock blue, purple and pink sewing threads

Method

Fold blue material in half. Cut out a front and back piece for the bag and a front piece for the belt.
Cut out a strip for the top of the bag.
Cut out a narrow strip 4 × 90 cm for the strap for the bag.
Cut out 4 strips 4 × 45 cm for the ties for the belt.
Cut out 5 lozenge shaped pieces for the belt from Lurex material.
Cut out 5 tree shaped pieces for the belt from purple fabric.
Cut out 8 pieces for the bag from the Lurex fabric.
Cut 54 cm purple bias binding for bag and 2 strips each 90 cm long for edging belt.

On each piece to be appliquéed iron lightweight Vilene on back. Turn under 1 cm round edge of each piece – clipping corners where necessary. Tack with contrast thread.

Bag

1 Back main pieces of peacock blue fabric with Vilene for bag and belt.
2 On front of bag slipstitch the Lurex pieces into place and the central shape of purple jap silk.
3 With right sides facing outwards sew bag together round edge using 3 mm seam allowance.

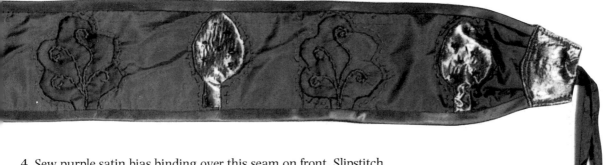

4 Sew purple satin bias binding over this seam on front. Slipstitch down at back.

5 Sew strip for top of bag at one end. Then match top width of bag with strip and with right sides together sew band on. Fold in half and sew down inside.

6 Attach straps onto each side of this band adding tassels on ends.

7 Embellish appliqué shapes with embroidery including stem stitch, running stitch and adding beads and sequins.

Belt

1 Mount appliqué shapes on top layer of fabric.

2 Place two layers of fabric together wrong sides facing.

3 Sew together with bias binding on the long edges, applying the binding first to the appliqué layer and then turning it over to the back and slipstitching.

4 Pleat ends of belt onto Lurex pieces and top stitch round shape securely by machine.

5 Sew two ties with attached tassels on each end of belt by hand stitching onto back.

3 Tie and dye

Introduction

Tie and dye is a method of obtaining a pattern by resist dyeing. Parts of the fabric are isolated so that they 'resist' colour when the fabric is immersed in dye. A number of techniques are used to isolate parts of the fabric. These include tying or binding, knotting, folding, plaiting, tritik and clamp resist, which can be used to create a wide variety of designs. These designs can be very complex and intricate or very bold and dramatic – and no two designs are ever alike. Tie and dye is often called 'plangi', the Malay word meaning spot, a characteristic of tie and dyed fabrics. The tie and dye process can be used to create monochrome designs or it can be repeated with different dye colours to create multicoloured and richly patterned designs.

Tie and dye is known almost all over the world and is one of the earliest forms of resist dyeing. This was probably because of the simplicity of its basic techniques. The earliest tie and dye fabric is believed to be Pre-Christian, first or second century B.C., from the Necropolis at Paracus in Peru. This fabric is woven from alpaca yarn with fringes on all sides. It is mainly brown with yellow, red and green spots, and could be a poncho as it is made up of two loom widths which have been partly joined. Also found in Peru, at Nazca, is a tie and dyed fragment, believed to be part of a poncho. This is made up entirely of a patchwork of 'L' shaped weaves, with an all over spot patterning. This simple patterning was typical of Pre-Columbian resist fabrics and was usually achieved by tying the rounded ends of wooden sticks before dyeing the fabric. The Pre-Columbians used indigo to create a variety of blue shades; cochineal for red and the bark of a pepper tree for yellow. Naturally these colours were mixed to create other colours. Pre-Columbian tie and dye fragments have been found in Arizona and New Mexico, in the U.S.A. Later, in the same region, tie and dye was practised by the Pueblo Indians who produced simple monochrome patterns of reserved circle or square designs which are still in use today.

Despite the early examples just described, evidence shows that tie and dye was a craft extensively practised in the East: in China, Japan and India. Tie and dye is believed to have fully developed in China between A.D. 617 and 906, during the T'ang Dynasty, encouraged by the first production of silk. From China craftsmen spread their skills of silk production (seri-culture) and weaving to Japan during the Nara Period between A.D. 646 and 794, influencing the style of dress by the introduction of tie and dyed fabrics. These fabrics were mainly worn by the nobility and priests. Early evidence of the practice of tie and dye in Japan has been found in twelfth century scrolls which tell us of the manners and customs of that time.

Early examples of tie and dye used silk. However by the sixteenth century cotton was being used and today soft leather is patterned by tie and dye for fashion accessories.

In India tie and dyed fabric is called Bandhani and is characterised by tiny spots and white circles. The fresco paintings of the Ajanta caves in Maharashtra, dating back to the sixth and seventh centuries, depict figures dressed in fabrics patterned in white circles.

In Europe tie and dye samples have been found in Hungary, practised by the Puszta tribe in the nineteenth century. They were nomadic herdsmen who used grasses, pebbles and seeds to create resist dyed indigo fabrics. Also samples have been found in Czechoslovakia and Sweden. In Russia tie and dye was a Jewish craft before the Russian Revolution of 1917.

Tie and dye has more recently become more popular in the West with the increasing interest in crafts from other cultures, and the popularity it found during the 1960s' Flower Power movement. Some of you may remember the tie-and-dyed T-shirts and dresses worn by hippies everywhere. Tie and dye was even used to decorate meditation tents, living rooms and mobile homes.

In the following pages you will be able to explore the rich variety of texture and colour of tie and dye. Tie and dye can be used to create attractive domestic furnishings such as cushions, tablecloths, and wall hangings.

Materials and equipment

Fabrics and materials for tying and binding

Cotton, silk, wool or synthetics can all be used for tie and dye. Most new woven fabrics have some finish or dressing on them and it is important to remove this. Wash the fabric in warm water using a natural liquid soap. Soda ash can be used to remove natural oils and finish. When you have washed the fabric, dry it thoroughly and iron it.

3:1 Samples of tying and binding.

The following materials can be used to tie and bind up areas of the fabric to isolate them from dye in different ways:

Threads – string, buttonhole thread, plastic twine, raffia, elastic bands, pipecleaners

Clamps – bulldog clips, paper clips or clothes pegs

Assortment of beans, pebbles, buttons, beads, coins, or even chick peas, lentils or rice for very fine circles

It is important to have a sharp pair of scissors or a seam unpicker to undo the knots and bindings.

Fabric marker pens are very useful for drawing patterns and the blue line they make is soluble in water. Charcoal pencils and sticks also make marks that are water soluble.

Dyes suitable for tie and dye and batik

A variety of dyes are suitable for tie and dye and batik. Dylon dyes are particularly popular in the U.K. as they are easy to use and are widely available from hardware shops, chemists, department stores and specialist craft shops. Vegetable dyes can also be used, but require a lot of experimenting to get satisfactory results.

Dylon Multi Purpose dyes

Dylon Multi Purpose dyes come in small tins and must be bought with a sachet of dye fixative.

Empty contents of tin of dye into a basin or jug. Mix with a small quantity of boiling water to form a paste. Add this mixture to the dyebath of water. Add one tablespoonful of common salt and a sachet of fixative per tin. Soak the fabric in cold water for a few minutes, wring out or blot excess water. Put into dyebath and simmer for 20 minutes stirring from time to time and remembering to keep fabric submerged at all times.

Dylon Liquid dyes

Add dye to hot water in dye bath, at the rate of one capful of dye and one tablespoonful of salt for every 5 oz weight of dry fabric.

Place fabric in dyebath and simmer for twenty minutes.

Dylon Cold dyes

Empty contents of tin into a jug or basin. Dissolve dye with enough hot water to form a paste. Mix four tablespoonfuls of salt and one sachet or fixative (or one tablespoonful of washing soda) with boiling water. Keep this mixture separate until it is time to immerse the fabric. The chemicals react instantly and a dyebath with soda added will only remain stable for about two hours. The two solutions can, however, be bottled and kept separately. When using cold dye the fabric needs to be submerged for about one hour to absorb all the dye.

Procion M Dyes – fibre reactive dyes

Procion M Dyes were developed by ICI Chemicals in the early part of the 1950s. They do not require heating or boiling as they work by adhering to the fabric by direct chemical linkage. This makes them easy to use. Procion M dyes are very fast in cold water and give bright colours to fabrics such as linen, calico and cotton, and slightly lighter results on wool and silk. This factor makes them ideal for use in batik. They can be easily mixed to create an infinite variety of colours.

Wash and Dye dyes
ICI chemicals have also produced excellent hot fast dyes specially designed for automatic washing machines. These are called 'Wash and Dye' and require a boil wash. Refer to dyeing instructions on the packet.

Dyes: Avoid ingestion, inhalation, and contact with eyes and skin. Keep out of reach of children and away from food. Wear rubber gloves, overalls and goggles when handling dyestuffs. Some type of facial filter mask should be worn. Store dyestuffs in closed containers, clearly labelled.

Equipment needed for dyeing
Containers for dyeing, dust mask for preparing dyes

Cold dyeing

Plastic buckets and bowls	Old saucepans
Sink and bath	Photographic trays

Hot dyeing
Enamel and metal saucepans, buckets and bowls
Rubber gloves to protect hands
Wooden or plastic tongs to stir and lift fabric out of dye bath
Newspaper, newsprint or brown paper to blot fabric
Sheet of pvc or polythene to cover worktop
Apron, old shirts or overalls to protect clothes from splashes of dye
Cleansing liquid, Swarfega, soap or barrier cream to prevent dye from
  staining the skin
Plastic, wooden or metal stirrers for stirring the dye bath
Plastic or metal spoons for measuring dye
Cooker or hot plate for hot dyeing.   Kettle

Washing machines are very useful for dyeing large quantities of fabric. It is important on completion of dyeing process to run your machine through a complete boil wash cycle using your normal washing powder and/or bleach to expel any remaining dye particles.

3:2 Materials and equipment for tie and dye: raffia, plastic twine, dye pot, Procion M and vat dyes, plastic bucket, rubber gloves, washing soda, salt, wooden tongs, string, metal spoons, tied fabric, etc.

Colours

Procion and Dylon dye colour chart

Procion M Colours	Dylon cold dyes	Colour
Brilliant Yellow M6G	A10 Primrose	lemon yellow
Yellow M4R	A18 Nasturtium	strong yellow
Brilliant Orange M2R	A27 Mandarin	bright orange red
Brilliant Red M8R	A16 Camellia	very strong bluish red good in pale shades
Scarlet MG	A14 Coral	scarlet, makes a rich brown mixed with
Blue M3G	A30 Turquoise	turquoise, attractive light shades good first blue in all blue schemes
Navy Blue M4R	A19 Purple Vine	bluish maroon, interesting dull pink in lighter shades
Olive Green M3G		good for toning

Mixing colours – basic colour combinations

red   + yellow = orange
red   + blue   = purple
yellow + blue   = green
purple + green = grey
purple + orange = brown
purple + blue   = indigo

Mixing Procion M

Black   1 part Brilliant Orange
         5 parts Blue
         OR
         5 parts Brilliant Red
         20 parts Yellow
         75 parts Navy Blue

Brown   1 part Blue
         5 parts Brilliant Orange

Recipe for Procion M Navy blue dye

3 tsps dye
4 tbsp salt dissolved in hot water
1 tbsp washing soda dissolved in hot water
4–5 litres of water for dye bath

Prepare tied cloth

3:3 Making and trimming the raffia ties.

Method
1 Pour cold water into bucket.
2 Dissolve dye with enough hot water to form a paste.
3 Add·dye to dye bath and stir well.
4 Place tied fabric into dye bath (see Soaking p. 59).

3:4 Preparing cold water dye bath. First stage: pouring hot water into bath.

3:5 Adding dye paste to dye bath.

3:6 Dyeing tied fabric.

5 Add salt and leave for 10 minutes.
6 Add washing soda and leave for 1 hour.
7 Remove fabric and rinse in cold water.
8 Undo the ties.
9 Wash in warm soapy water.

3:7 Unpicking the raffia ties.

Approximate quantities of fabric to Dylon dye

Multipurpose dyes
2–3 m² of medium weight fabric to one tin of dye

Liquid dyes
8–10 m² of medium weight fabric for one plastic bottle of dye

Cold water dyes
2–3 ² of medium weight fabric per tin
Vat dyes
Synthetic dyes

Techniques

Basic sequence of operations

Binding
Binding the fabric with thread or otherwise is the first important part of the tie and dye process. The tighter the binding and tying the greater the resist.

Soaking
The fabric must be wet before it is dyed to ensure a sharp colour contrast. Soak fabric when bound up, remove excess water by dabbing fabric on paper.

Dyeing
Put into the dyebath. Remember to keep the fabric well submerged and gently agitate so that it dyes evenly.

Rinsing
When the fabric has been dyed rinse in cold water until the water runs clear.

Dyeing with more than one colour
If a second or third colour is desired remember that the colours are additive, eg, first dye yellow, second dye red, result = orange. Always start with the lightest colour and either refold and retie the bindings between dyebaths or add new bindings in different places. The new bindings will resist the next dyeing.

Fixing
Immerse dyed fabric in hot water alternately with cold rinses. This enriches and fixes dye to fabric at the same time. A hot iron also fixes dye to fabric. Do not use a hot iron on synthetics as this can leave scorch marks. Alternatively put the dyed fabric in a tumble dryer and set at a temperature appropriate to the fabric used. This is ideal when large quantities of fabric have been dyed.

Simple techniques

Bulldog clips
1 Fold fabric by concertina pleating to form a rectangle (*3:8*).
2 Use a warm iron to flatten the pleats.
3 Position bulldog clips diagonally to create a chevron pattern (*3:9*).

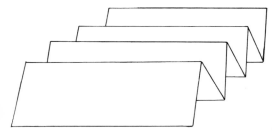

3:8 Fold fabric.

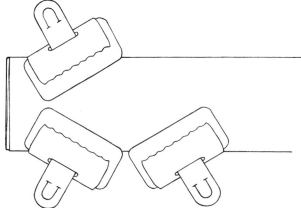

3:9 Position bulldog clips diagonally to edge of fabric.

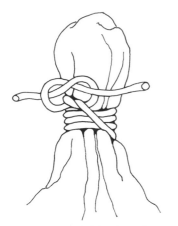

3:10 Tie fabric and finish with a reef knot.

Random tying

1 Draw up fabric using finger tips.

2 Hold and tie at varying distances from the edge (*3:10* and *3:11*).

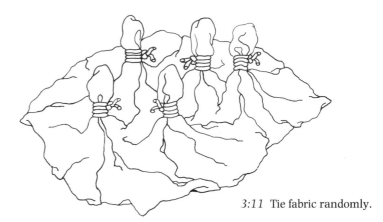

3:11 Tie fabric randomly.

Pegs

1 Fold fabric by concertina pleating to form a rectangle (*3:8*).

2 Use a warm iron to flatten the pleats.

3 Attach bottom right hand corner of folded fabric to top edge of polythene strip, forming an equilateral triangle (*3:12*).

4 Hold fabric and polythene in place by clipping two pegs parallel to each other along folded edge.

5 Wrap fabric round the polythene strip placing pegs in alternating sequence of twos and threes with each wrap.

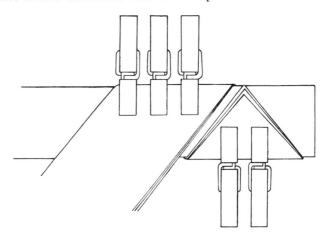

3:12 Wrap fabric round a strip of rigid polythene.

Rolled and tied

1 Fold fabric in half and half again (*3:13*).

2 Tightly roll fabric from corner to the corner diagonally opposite (*3:14*).

3 Bind and tie at regular intervals beginning from the centre (*3:16*).

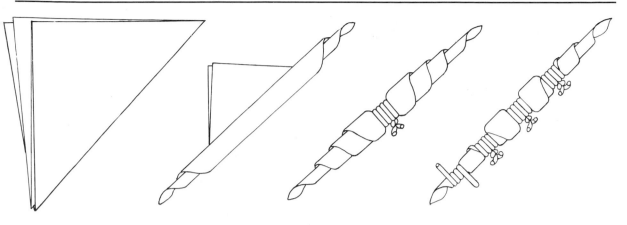

3:13 Fold fabric into a square and then a triangle.

3:14 Roll long folded edge across to opposite corner diagonally.

3:15 Tie tightly at the centre first.

3:16 Make ties at intervals, working from the centre outwards.

Overstitch

1 Fold fabric horizontally to form a rectangle (*3:17*).

2 Use a hot iron to flatten in place.

3 Pin through all fabric to secure layers.

4 Draw pattern on fabric using a soft pencil or fabric pen.

5 Thread up a thickish but pointed needle, using a strong thread, for example button thread. Make a double knot at end of thread.

6 Stab needle through all layers of fabric starting from a corner.

7 Overstitch along horizontal edges first pulling thread tightly as you go along (*3:18*).

8 To overstitch the vertical and diagonal lines fold fabric along these lines and continue to overstitch as before.

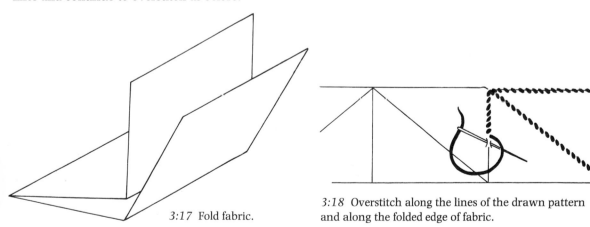

3:17 Fold fabric.

3:18 Overstitch along the lines of the drawn pattern and along the folded edge of fabric.

Ruching

1 Roll fabric tightly round cord beginning at one corner and working towards the diagonally opposite corner (*3:19*).

2 It is important that you leave at least 5 cm of cord at both ends of rolled fabric.

3 Holding rolled fabric securely draw both cords together gradually, gathering up the fabric until tight and the fabric forms a circle (*3:20*).

4 Tie a reef knot to secure the gathered fabric (*3:21*).

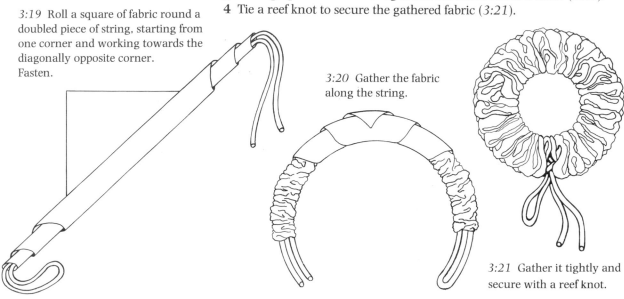

3:19 Roll a square of fabric round a doubled piece of string, starting from one corner and working towards the diagonally opposite corner. Fasten.

3:20 Gather the fabric along the string.

3:21 Gather it tightly and secure with a reef knot.

machine-stitched tritik   *clump tied*   *rolled and tied*   *overstitched*

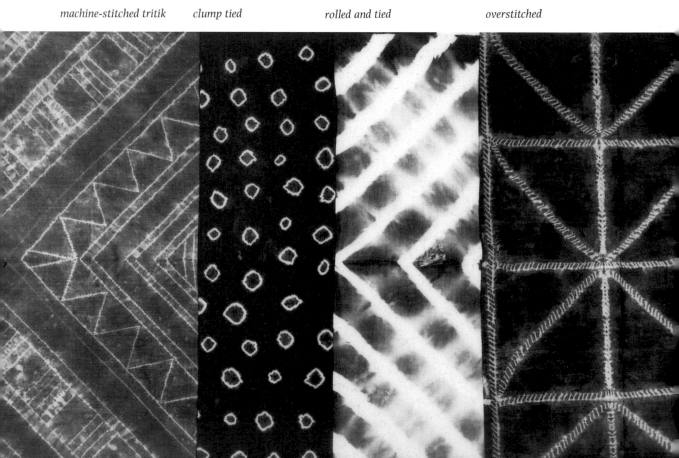

Marbling
1 Crumple the fabric into a ball.
2 Bind very tightly with string or other suitable thread in a random fashion. A small amount of binding will allow more dye to penetrate.
3 After the first colour is dyed, undo the string and retie the fabric, and dye a second colour.

Clump tying
1 Tie in small pebbles, beans, coins, shells or buttons. These can be tied at random or can follow a more regular pattern which can be pre-drawn onto the fabric.
2 Make each tie using a continuous piece of thread as this will make it easier to untie after dyeing.

Knotting
The best results in knotting are achieved with fine fabrics.
1 Roll, pleat or leave single the fabric and knot it on itself. The knots can be reinforced with extra binding of thread to achieve an interesting resist.
2 This method can create more effective patterns if after the first dyeing the knots are undone and the fabric is retied and dyed in another colour.

3:22 Selection of tie and dye cotton cloths.

hand-stitched tritik   *bulldog clips*   *ruching*   *pegs*

Examples of different effects

Circles

These can be achieved by tying found objects such as stones, marbles, buttons and beans into the fabric. Alternatively the fabric can be drawn up into small or large peaks, bound with thread.

Sunbursts

This effect is created by starting from the centre of the fabric, picking up the fabric to form a central peak. The fabric is then arranged evenly round the centre and bound at intervals to form concentric circles of resist.

Stripes

There are several methods of dyeing fabric to achieve stripes. Pleat or roll the fabric into a tube lengthways for vertical stripes. Pleat horizontally for horizontal pleats. For diagonal stripes pleat diagonally. When pleated bind the fabric at intervals. If narrow stripes are desired fold fabric into narrow pleats and make wider pleats for broader stripes. It is best to iron the pleats to make the folds really crisp.

Further techniques

Reverse tie and dye

If a reverse effect is required, for example to produce a white pattern on a dark fabric then use either a commercial colour and stain remover such as Dygon or ordinary domestic bleach which has similar effect. When using Dygon dissolve one capful of Dygon powder to 500 g of material and $\frac{1}{2}$ litre of boiling water. Simmer bound fabric for 10 minutes. If using bleach the fabric is first dyed then put into a solution of 5 parts water to 1 part bleach and leave for about 10 minutes. If you are going to use commercially dyed fabric, do a test piece first with bleach or Dygon before commencing on a large piece. Dygon is not recommended on non-fast dyed fabrics, acrylics or polyester. Always wash fabric very thoroughly after using Dygon or bleach as otherwise the fabric will in time disintegrate. Dygon comes with its own instructions for use.

Asymmetric designs

Fold fabric in any direction and dip dye corners or edges. This will create a pattern that is more defined at these points. Refold and redye if you wish to build up more pattern and colour.

Stencils

Stencils can be used to create attractive single motif designs or more elaborate repeat patterns. Cut a stencil design out of solid wood, plastic or metal. Clamp tightly together one or more layers of fabric and the stencil between boards. 'G' clamp(s) can be used and are available at most DIY shops.

Submerge in dyebath using hot or cold dyes. Do not boil dyebath when using plastic (or such low melt point materials) for the stencil. Remove from dyebath when you have the colour you require. Rinse, wash and dry. Reclamp and redye if additional design motifs are to be introduced and another colour used.

Plate 12 Tie and dye appliqué wall hanging by Mary Spyrou, inspired by Coptic wall tiles. A combination of random tying, stitch resist and running stitch.

Plate 13 Cushion by Mary Spyrou and bows by Margo Singer. Cushion and cerise silk bows produced by a combination of resist techniques with bulldog clips and pegs. Blue and copper-coloured silk bows produced by a combination of folding and tying, and sunbursts.

Plate 14 Indigo-dyed cotton cloths from Nigeria and Sierra Leone (Etha Brandon). A combination of tie dye and stitch resist.

Plate 15 Detail of a tritik cotton robe from Sierra Leone by Etha Brandon. Etha wearing a tritik robe from Sierra Leone. Chain-stitched yoke.

Tritik

Tritik refers to the use of stitching to create resist patterns. The beauty of tritik is that you can create drawn images on fabric, with shapes such as circles, squares, triangles, chevrons, parallel lines, lettering, pictorial designs and freer, more abstract designs. This gives you more control over the final result than by tying and binding fabric, which have been described earlier in the chapter.

Tritik patterns are achieved by the use of close running stitches to outline the design and to pick out precise details. A variety of fabrics can be used. Closely-woven fabrics such as silk and cotton lawn are particularly suitable though open weaves such as muslin can create interesting effects, (*Plate 12*). The basic process is common to all tritik with some variations. This is as follows:

Use fabric single, double or folded several times depending on how much of a repeat design you want. If you want just a single motif design, use a single layer of fabric.

Draw your design onto the fabric using a soft pencil, fabric pen or by transferring your original design with dressmaker's carbon paper and a tracing wheel.

To hand or overstitch your design choose a strong thread, for example button or gimp; for machine tritik, a polyester cotton.

For hand and overstitch tritik, use either single or double thread depending on the thickness of outline you want. Thread up a sewing needle, preferably fairly thick with a fine point, for example a crewel needle which is commonly used in embroidery. The finer the point the easier it is to stitch through the layers of fabric and fewer holes will be visible in the finished fabric. It is important that the thread has a double knot at the end before you begin to stitch. Use close and even running stitches for hand tritik and whipping stitch for overstitch tritik.

When doing machine tritik set the tension mechanism as loose as possible and the stitch length dial on no.4. Running or zigzag is suitable for machine tritik.

Remember to leave sufficient length of thread to pull. Finally gather up your fabric. Continue to draw up the fabric until no thread is visible and the fabric is tightly gathered. Reinforce thread by backstitching over and over again at the end on the same spot. This is important to avoid thread slackening and fabric coming apart.

Dye fabric (see pages 54 to 58). Cut ends of gathering thread with a pair of scissors or a stitch unpicker. The fabric will become unravelled.

Wash in soapy water. Rinse and dry in a well ventilated place, avoiding direct sunlight. Iron.

Tritik (hand stitch)
1 See overstitch 1–6 (page 61).
2 Stitch fabric using close and even running stitches (*3:23*).
3 Leave at least 2.5 cm of thread at the end of your stitching.
4 Pull thread tightly.
5 Make a double knot to prevent drawn fabric from becoming undone.

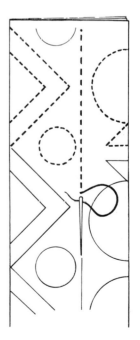

3:23 Sew along the lines of the design with running stitch.

Tritik (machine stitch)

1 Fold fabric in half and half again (*3:24*).

2 Iron flat with a warm iron.

3 Pin fabric through all layers to keep layers in place.

4 Draw pattern using a fabric pen or soft charcoal pencil and ruler.

5 Thread up machine choosing a thick machine needle (size 100) and a strong thread such as polyester buttonhole thread.

6 Set stitch length dial at '4' and loosen the tension.

7 Reverse stitch at the start of machining the pattern. It is important to leave at least 5 cm of thread at the end of each stitching line. Sew along drawn pattern (*3:25*).

8 Pull thread very carefully, easing fabric along with the tips of your fingers until all the fabric is gathered up tightly.

9 Secure ends with a double knot.

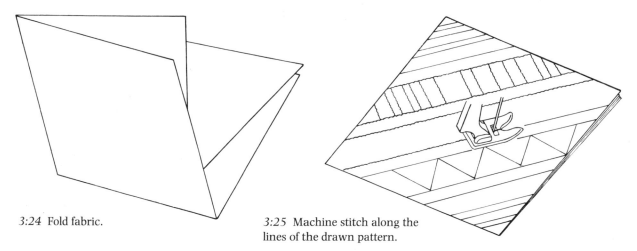

3:24 Fold fabric.

3:25 Machine stitch along the lines of the drawn pattern.

Projects

Tie and dyed bow project

The tie and dyed bows (*Plate 13*) were made from silk satin but can also be made from other types of fine silk, cotton or polyester.

The fabric is first washed (see instructions p. 53). Then cut the fabric to measure 26 × 22 cm.

The techniques used to decorate the bows are as follows; see instructions on pages 59 to 63.

1 Pink bow – bulldog clips
2 Blue bow – tied with thread
3 Ochre bow – bulldog clips and clothes pegs
4 Brown bow – tied with thread
5 Green bow – tied with thread

When deciding on the technique for any sort of bow, bear in mind that the bow will be gathered into the centre and the band will cover some of the central area of the bow. So the design should show up more on the outside. If the visible part of the design is not too complex, then the actual band which goes around the centre can be patterned, or dyed in another colour. If more complexity and richness of design are required, it is better to tie and dye the fabric twice.

This is particularly easy to do with bulldog clips or clothes pegs as these can be easily removed and repositioned.

Making up the bows
The bows can be made directly with the dyed fabric. If a firmer appearance is desired the fabric can be stiffened by ironing onto it a piece of lightweight iron-on Vilene, cut 2 cm smaller all round. This should be done after the fabric has been tie and dyed, washed, rinsed, dried and ironed flat.

The square fabric for the bow is folded then sewn round three sides leaving an opening of about 3.4 cm (*3:26*). The opening allows the fabric to be turned inside out. Before turning the fabric, remember to clip the corners to allow the fabric to be ironed flat on the right side.

3:26 Fold silk with right sides together. Sew but leave an opening.

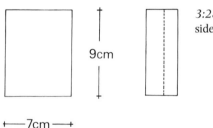

9cm

⊢—7cm—⊣

3:27 Small piece of silk for the centre of the bow.

3:28 Fold with right sides together and sew.

3:29 Turn inside out.

Cut a small piece of fabric 9 × 7 cm for the band (*3:27*). This can also be backed by Vilene. Fold lengthwise and sew with a normal 1.5 cm seam allowance. Turn inside out. The right side now facing you forms a narrow band 9 cm long (*3:28*). Sew one end with 1.5 cm seam (*3:29*). Turn inside out and slip over the bow to form a central band. Attach a hairclip to the back of the bow by sewing it on by hand (*3:30*), or a piece of narrow elastic can be used if the bow is to be used as a bow tie.

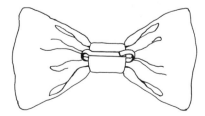

3:30 Bow seen from the back to show the clip.

Cushion project

The cushion plate B is made up simply of strips of tie and dyed fabric. Only two colours are used, bulldog clips and pegs to create the overall pattern on the front of the cushion, the back is plain with a zip in the centre back.

Materials
1 m of cotton lawn or silk (with extra for seaming the tie and dyed strips together)
2 m of bias binding and piping cord
35 cm lightweight zip
A pair of dressmaking scissors, a tape measure, pins, tailor's chalk and a reel of sewing thread (Try to select a thread which will match overall the variety of colours in your tie and dyed fabric.
Large metal bulldog clips and wooden pegs (Plastic pegs and bulldog clips can also be used though the results are less satisfactory and cannot be boiled)

Method
1 Wash and prepare fabric, (see page 53).
2 Cut a piece of fabric 52 × 52 cm to make the back of the cushion. Cut a generous 2.30 m strip for the piping (see instructions). With the remaining fabric cut five strips of 6 × 52 cm and five strips of 7 × 52 cm.
3 Follows instructions for dyeing the fabric (see page 57). Two dyebaths, brilliant red and turqouise blue, were used, the red in small quantity to achieve the pink. The dye bath will remain active for approximately two hours. This can be used for the second dyeing.
  Dye the narrow strips and the back piece turquoise and the wider strips and piping pink.
4 Fold each strip across the narrow width.
5 Iron with a hot iron to flatten into a more or less square shape.
6 Use a combination of pegs and bulldog clips to form asymmetric patterns of your choice (*3:9* and *3:12*).
7 Dye the folded and clamped pink fabric in the light turquoise dyebath and the light turquoise fabric in the red dye bath.
8 When the strips have been dyed, dried and ironed take alternative strips of patterned pink and turquoise fabric. Pin together along the long edge and tack. Continue doing this until all the strips are tacked together (*3:31*).
9 Sew 1 cm from the edge. You will be left with alternating stripes of pink and turquoise patterns.
10 Iron seams flat.
11 The striped fabric should measure 52 cm square.
12 To make piping (see page 109). Use the dyed pink fabric.
13 Pin piping to the front of the cushion, easing carefully round each corner, mitring at the corners of the cushion to enable the corners to lie flat.
14 Make up piped cushion (see page 115). Completed size 50 cm square.

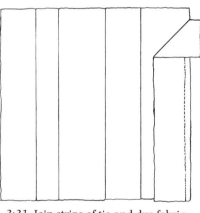

3:31 Join strips of tie and dye fabric with the right sides together.

World survey

India

In India, tie and dyed fabrics are called bandhani. They are widely produced and worn in the North West States of Gujarat and Rajasthan. The
designs and colours of bandhani are linked with social and religious customs. Tie and dye is also practised in South Madras where a small community from Gujarat has settled.

Bandhani are traditionally made of fine silk, muslin or wool which is
folded many times, dampened and then pressed over a pin board where
pins are arranged in a particular design. The tying is done both by men
and women. The dyeing is a male occupation using both vegetable and
chemical dyes.

The most highly prized bandhani in Gujarat is the gharchola, the wedding sari, which is essential to a bride's dowry. There are two important
designs, the bar bagh or bavan bagh (12–52 gardens), a very appropriate
name as when the sari is spread out it has the appearance of a garden in
full bloom. Amongst the wealthy, bandhani often have gold squares of
dotted patterns. More commonly they are dyed red to bring good fortune,
made up a squares forming diagonal patterns across the fabric. Within
each square is a motif of an elephant, flower, or doll. The pallu (the sari end
which falls over the shoulder at the back) and the border has a traditional
design called a veer bhat. A bhat means gift and a veer means brother, for a
veer bhat is a gift from a brother to a sister. A very traditional gharchola is
dyed leaf green with circles and diagonal dotted squares covering the
entire fabric.

Typical of Bhuj and Jamnagar (in Gujarat) are bandhani with matching
or contrasting borders and pallus. They have designs of small dots and
circles as the amba dal and choki dal which have simple square designs of
dots, the morzad which is composed of peacocks, the basant baher which is
a rich display of flowers symbolic of spring, and the kodidana and khand
bhat which are simple designs of dots in a variety of traditional colours of
red, green, yellow, blue and black. Unusual colour combinations of pink
and grey, pink and violet, peacock blue and black are also frequent.

In Rajasthan, the state bordering Gujarat to the north, bandhani are
also popular. Women dressed in saris and wraps and men in turbans of
many colours are a common sight. Contrasting shades of red and yellow
are particularly favoured. On sale in the market place can be found par-
tially tied and bound sari and turban lengths revealing the design. Particular bandhani designs and colours are used for certain festivals, seasons and
rituals. Bandhani are sometimes identified by their style of dyeing: the
dorookha is in two colours, one on each side; the lahariya has diagonally
arranged coloured stripes, often further distinguished by the number of
colours used (eg, pancharangi has five, satrangi has seven). Rajasthani
bandhani are made with elaborate arrangements of ties which produce
dotted designs of leaves and creepers, animals and birds, dancing figures
and geometric designs. The men design, the women tie. The dyeing process in Rajasthan is a little different. Firstly the base colour is dyed, then the
areas which are to retain this colour are tied. Other areas are daubed with
a variety of colours, which are also tied. The fabric is then washed and any
area of colour which has been left untied is washed away.

Traditionally natural dyes such as the curcuma, indigo, cochineal and safflower were used. However, by 1900 aniline dyes largely replaced natural dyes and since 1945 reactive dyes are widely used.

Indonesia

Characteristic of Java is the tie and dyed fabric called kembangan. The kembangen was traditionally worn as a court costume called a dodot but nowadays tends to be worn as a shoulder shawl or slendang. It has a large resist central panel, usually oblong, diamond or ellipse shaped, edged with tritik. It is often richly coloured in violet, red, gold or blue and sometimes combined with batik and hand painting.

Other styles of tie and dye fabrics are important in Palembang, South East Sumatra, Java and Bali. These are worn as shawls, sashes and breast wraps, which are also important as accessories to dance costumes. Motifs of paisley, crosses and rosette designs result from a combination of tying and tritik.

Japan

In Japan tie and dye is known as shibori. There are a variety of shibori techniques characteristic of particular regions. For example, Kyo shibori from Kyoto uses minute ties to create precise patterns whereas, in contrast, yukata shibori from Narumi and Arimatsu incorporates bold patterns on indigo blue cotton.

The early use of the clamp resist method was practised in the Nara period and is still practised today. This involves the use of patterned wooden blocks. The design is carved deeply to provide channels in the design, an important feature as this enables the dye to circulate when the fabric and block are clamped closely together. This method tends to give the design a soft outline. Clamp resist techniques are often combined with others such as embroidery, hand painting and batik.

Okejime shibori is another interesting method where fabric or yarn is partly placed in a bucket, a lid is secured on top leaving the excess fabric or yarn hanging outside. This fabric is then tied and dyed. Rope tying, folding and stitching are other methods also used in Japan to create resist patterns.

West Africa

In West Africa the wealth, class and status of the wearer have often been distinguished by the artistic quality of the resist dyed fabric, and regional characteristics are evident.

The Yoruba women of Nigeria use a combination of tying, pleating, rope tying, sewing (tritik) and found objects (beads, small stones and seeds) to create richly textured fabrics known as adire eleso (see *Plate 14* and *3:32*). The Yoruba women then dye their fabrics in large earthenware pots while the men and children do the finishing process. This involves folding and beating the fabric repeatedly until the cloth is supple and shiny. Often indigo is beaten directly into the dyed fabric. This gives it a coppery burnished look which makes it more valuable. Amongst the Yoruba indigo and other sources of colour are believed to have supernatural qualities, relating to religion, myths, legends and folktales. Indigo dyeing is closely linked with the goddess called Iya Mapo, the protector of all female trades. Worship, celebrations and the bringing of offerings interrupt these activities.

In other parts of Nigeria the dyeing process is done by men, as in Kano where circular deep cement pits are used. However, nowadays chemically produced synthetic vat dyes are commonly used, imported from northern Europe, along with printed fabrics that imitate tie and dye. They are even printed not to be colour fast so the colour bleeds to give the fabric a 'genuine' appearance and stains the skin and other clothing.

3:32 Indigo-dyed cloth with regular pattern of tying, from Nigeria (Yoruba). (Etha Brandon)

3:33 and *3:34* Tritik cloths from Senegal (Charles Beving Collection).

Further along the coast of West Africa are Senegal and Sierra Leone where tritik was commonly used to pattern striped and brocaded cottons, imported from Europe towards the end of the nineteenth century and still used today. Two fine examples (*3:33* and *3:34*) were brought back to England in the nineteenth century by Beving, a textile factory owner, who collected textiles from West Africa and the East to imitate in his factory. They are both made up of two widths of brocaded sateen, dyed indigo. The elaborate designs were produced by tritik.

More recent examples of tritik are those illustrated in *Plate 15*, made by Etha Brandon from Sierra Leone. The detail shows one tritik robe; the robe worn by Etha has a chain stitched yoke.

In the Ivory Coast raffia was traditionally tie and dyed and made into cloth.

4 Batik

Introduction

Batik, like tie and dye, is a resist technique. It uses the application of hot wax as a resist so that when dyed only the unwaxed areas accept the colour. Other mediums with similar properties to wax, and traditionally used, are, for example, cassava paste, clay, mud and soya cheese. Batik has been used traditionally to effect patterns on fabric but the technique was also used by the Pre Columbians to pattern pots before glazing and firing. Indeed this practice is still used by many potters all over the world. In Eastern Europe, eggs are decorated for festive occasions by fine drawing in wax followed by dyeing.

The word batik comes from Indonesia and means 'wax writing'. Indonesia is world famous for its fine and elaborate batik fabrics which are traditionally produced on the island of Java. The skills involved in batik are extremely high and tend to be passed on through the generations of a family.

The origins of batik are uncertain because like so many textiles they disintegrate in a humid environment. Early batik fragments have been discovered in Egyptian tombs dating back to first century A.D. Fragments from the fifth century necropolis of Sakkara were discovered at Achmin. They depicted the Annunciation and were probably the work of the Copts. Other examples, believed to be wall hangings and altar covers, show white patterns on a blue ground depicting Biblical scenes. A small cotton batik banner found near Fostat, near Cairo, dates back to 1230–1350 and shows the use of indigo on white. It is believed to be Coptic but may have originated in Gujurat, India.

In the Nara period of Japan A.D. 646–794, a period of Japan's history that was influenced by Chinese crafts, wax resist was practised and was known as 'rokechi'. An early example of Chinese wax resist (part of a court screen) was discovered in a Japanese tomb.

Excavations in north-west China have uncovered monochrome fabrics in blue on white and red on white, patterned with floral motifs, resembling the designs of silks from the Nara period. These designs were probably made with stencils or blocks.

Some theories suggest that batik originated in China, spreading to Japan and then eastwards. A fragment of resist fabric dating from A.D. 1100–1200 depicting brown figures, influenced by the Tihuanaco culture from the Middle Inca period was discovered in Peru.

It is certainly believed that batik was native to the Indian Sub-continent. Traditionally the south east coast of India from the Deccan plateau to Cape Comorin was famous for its batik cloths. In Madras in the fifteenth century the tjap was developed and widely used. Being well situated on the coast provided ideal export outlet. Unfortunately batik practice has largely disappeared in India replaced mainly by imitation printed batiks. It is said that batik was introduced to Java in the twelfth century by the Indians who came to settle there and through early trading links.

During the thirteenth century batik was only practised by the ladies of the Sultan's family and the courts in the Royal areas of central Java. Here particular designs began to be identified with particular families. These batiks were soon in such demand that more and more people were being involved in their production and they were no longer confined to the courts. By the seventeenth century batiks were in widespread use. They even gained popularity in Europe, through the increase in trade with the East Indies Company. Batiks began to be commissioned from Europe which led to the introduction of new designs.

Today Java and the neighbouring islands of Sumatra and Bali are the most important batik producing areas.

In West Africa paste resist is more common than wax, and indigo the most common dye. Amongst the Yoruba of Nigeria cassava paste resists are hand drawn by women using a chicken feather, brush or vein of a palm leaf, while metal stencils cut from sheet zinc are made and used by men to apply the patterns. Mill cottons imported from Europe are mainly used, either plain or sometimes even patterned. The designs are symbolic, figurative and geometric and are often used for festivals, marriages and coronations. Very large cloths are often used as wallhangings. Typical of the Ivory Coast is the application of paste all over the cloth which when dried is scraped away often using a comb to create zigzag patterns and straight lines.

Following the arrival of batiks in the Netherlands in the seventeenth century, through trading links with South East Asia and West Africa, European textile manufacturers began to imitate Africa and Javanese batik designs by printing them, initially with copper rollers and natural dyes. With the introduction of synethetic dyes in the late nineteenth century, production increased. Even the crackled effect that characterised so many batiks was being imitated. In Manchester, the Netherlands, Switzerland and Germany batiks were commercially produced. The Art Nouveau period at the turn of the century greatly influenced batik design. The development of the electrically heated tjanting further encouraged the production of batiks. By the 1920s batiks were being worn as fashion garments. Unfortunately because of the slump in the textile industry in Europe in the 1920s, batik production ended. Interest in batik clothing revived in the 1930s thanks to the exposure by Hollywood celebrities and to the development of wider air and sea travel to South-East Asia. Since the end of World War II Indonesia has revitalised its batik production, supported and funded by the government. A batik research institute called the Wastraprema Society was established in 1976 which has a comprehensive collection of batik designs and cloth.

Although batik has almost disappeared as a craft in Europe, resist printed indigo fabrics using paste are still being made by some skilled crafts people in Czechoslovakia, in the rural villages of Moravia and Slovakia. Costumes with finely pleated skirts, aprons and head scarves are decorated with images of fruit, foliage and flowers inspired by the natural environment. The most commonly used colours are white and coloured images on a deep indigo ground.

Imitation batiks can be seen for sale in the East End of London, the main clothing trade area of the city. Many of these have been imported from Holland and bear the wax mark, the supposed sign of a 'genuine' batik. The designs reflect twentieth century Western images, regarded as having important status by many people who come from Africa and beyond to buy them.

These images include cars, money, aeroplanes and ships all of them the result of the oil boom, which has altered traditional values and lifestyles and has resulted in the replacing of many of the traditional symbols and designs mentioned earlier.

Materials and equipment

Fabrics suitable for batik

For the best results choose a fine natural fabric as this is the most absorbent of the hot wax and cold dyes. Use silk, cotton lawn, cotton, linen, muslin, old pillow slips and sheets. Avoid using synthetics and drip dry fabrics as these are less absorbent to the hot wax and cold dyes.

4:1 Materials and equipment for batik and direct fabric painting: iron, urea, soda ash, saucepan, soda crystals, measuring jug, small basin, electric tjanting, shallow tray, Procion M dyes, washing tongs, wax, variety of brushes, measuring batik frame, charcoal sticks and Deka dyes.

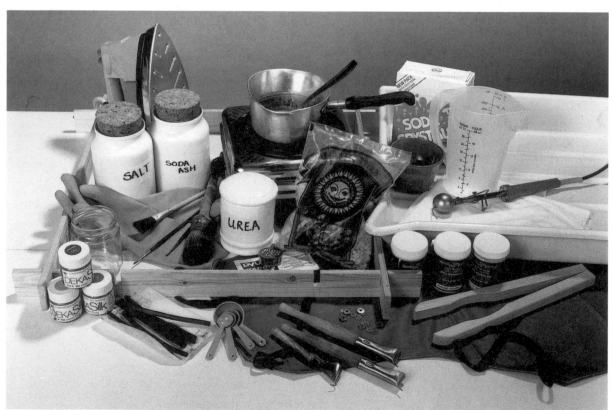

Wax for resist

Candles   Beeswax
Paraffin wax   Batik wax (50% beeswax and 50% paraffin wax)

Candles can be melted down and used in combination with beeswax. Paraffin wax produces a good crackle effect, one of the effects characteristic of batiks (beeswax is too soft). Candles and paraffin wax can be bought in most hardware shops. Paraffin wax comes in slabs which can be easily broken up with a hammer. Batik wax can be bought from specialist shops or from suppliers to candle makers in pre-packed bags of fine granules or 'split pea' size pieces. This is the ideal way of buying wax for resist dyeing, as it quickly melts on contact with heat.

Heating the wax

Warning: Treat hot wax with great care. Best of all use a wax pot, thermostatically controlled with a regulator. Alternatively you can use a saucepan and thermometer. Never put a saucepan over a fierce flame. Place on an electric hotplate with an adjustable thermostat control on a flat work surface.

A suitable and safe container to heat the wax is essential as this can otherwise be dangerous. A double boiler pan such as a porridge pan or bain-marie will be adequate. These are pans within a pan: you put the wax in the inner pan and water in the outer pan. Place on a constant low heat, on either a cooker or, ideally, an electric hotplate on a flat work surface. A batik pot or waterless kettle are ideal but they can be expensive. An electric glue pot with a thermostat control is a useful substitute. Always make sure that the room is well ventilated as the wax can give off fumes.

Never allow the water to be more than halfway up the outside of a wax container, as any contact the wax may have with the water will result in the wax spitting outwards. This can result in severe burns. It is important to keep the wax at a constant temperature, simmering at approximately 170° Fahrenheit. Keep the thermometer close at hand to check the temperature of the wax. Never allow it to overheat or the water level to drop as the wax can become inflamed, much like fat in a frying pan. Always top up the water regularly. Should wax ignite by accident have a damp cloth, a fire blanket or a container of dry baking soda handy to smother the flames. Do not use water to put out flames as this will cause the wax to spit and to become inflamed.

Tjantings

Tjantings are tools for drawing with wax, much like a pen. They originated from Java. A tjanting has a wooden handle like that of a dip pen, with a metal (usually copper) rounded wax holder at one end which looks like an elongated head with a short spout. Hot wax is put in the holder and fed through the spout onto the fabric. Tjantings come in a variety of designs and sizes, with single, double or triple spouts of different thickness. They can be bought from specialist craft suppliers.

The electric tjanting is a recent invention. It is basically the adaptation of a traditional tjanting to electricity with its own in-built thermostat.

It is simple to use and a direct method of designing batik without having to set up a wax pot. The wax is kept at a constant temperature and therefore flows fairly evenly. There is little wax wasted. Another advantage is the tjanting's portability and the fact that it does not give off as many fumes as a wax pot. A new adaptation of the electric tjanting is the batik funnel pen with a pencil type soldering iron attachment. Easy to use batik wax can be heated quickly maintaining an even melting temperature.

Tjaps

In Java metal stamps known as tjaps are used to create repeat designs. They were introduced in response to a demand for batik fabrics in the West, towards the end of the nineteenth century.

These stamps can be easily made with metal scrap. Mechanical components from old bicycles and clocks can be mounted on a stick (which forms a handle) or held with a pair of pliers. Nails, nuts and bolts, corks, cut potatoes and lino blocks can also be used for stamps. Imaginative designs can be created by combining several of such objects as one stamp.

Dyes

See information on dyes in the chapter on tie and dye, page 54.

Waxing techniques

Brushed wax

Wax can be used to create a variety of patterns and textures.

An interesting method of creating a picture in wax is to stretch a plain piece of fabric (closely woven cotton works best) on a frame. With a large decorator's brush cover the whole surface of the fabric with a layer of wax. Use large brush strokes across the surface. Take the material off the frame and turn it over. Brush wax over this side, too, making sure that the whole surface is covered. When the wax has solidified, sketch a design on the first waxed surface by scraping away the wax to reveal the fabric beneath. Use the point of compasses, a blunt needle, a knife, fork or screwdriver. Turn the fabric over to the back to make sure that where the wax has been scraped away on one side the fabric is also free from wax on the other side.

Then you can either immerse the waxed design in a dyebath or paint the fabric with dye. The dye will only seep into the areas that have been scraped free of wax.

Dripped wax

Dripping hot wax directly onto a piece of fabric can produce interesting abstract designs. Either stretch a piece of fabric onto a frame to tape it down on a sheet of greaseproof paper. Take a brush, stick or tjanting. Dip a tool such as a wooden stick or tube into the hot wax and then hold over the fabric, dripping wax at random. Try to draw a design in 'space'. Dye in a dyebath or paint the fabric with dyes. The process can be repeated dripping from a height to build up pattern and colour.

Crackling technique

The crackle effect is very characteristic of batik designs. Cover the fabric thoroughly with wax and allow to cool. Then crumple up the fabric in your hand before submerging it in the dyebath (*4:15*). One way of ensuring crips crackled lines is to put the waxed fabric in the refrigerator or freezer for about an hour before crumpling. Paraffin wax gives the most effective crackle as it is more brittle than batik wax or beeswax. If you want a more subtle crackle effect, use beeswax. If you want a pattern of straight lines, then fold the waxed fabric carefully instead of crumpling. Try folding the fabric vertically, diagonally or horizontally.

Tjanting work
For examples of fine tjanting work by Pat Hodson, see *Plate 21*.

Using stamps (or tjaps)
Tjaps wax both sides of the fabric (*4:2*). This is a much quicker way of creating fine designs on fabric than using the traditional tjanting method.

4:2 Examples of modern Indonesian batiks (tjap techniques used for the upper three). (Kate Dean and Sally Coombes)

Tjap designs are usually intricate and made of metal, usually of copper strips fixed to a frame with a handle on the back. The tjaps are dipped in wax and then the wax is stamped onto the fabric in repeat, usually on both sides of the fabric. After the first dyeing the wax is removed where the dye is to penetrate. A second waxing follows. This process is repeated until the design has been completed. The advantage of using a metal stamp is that the wax remains in a liquid state until it reaches the fabric.

Removing wax

Wax can be removed in a number of ways. It can be first scraped off using a blunt instrument such as a palette knife which will remove the top layer of wax. As this method does not completely remove the wax, iron fabric between sheets of newsprint or brown paper (4:3). Change the paper when it becomes soaked with wax and continue this process until most of the wax is removed (4:4). The fabric will probably still be stiff. Plunge fabric into a bowl of boiling water. Keep submerged for several minutes. This will

4:3 Ironing dried fabric between sheets of newsprint to remove wax.

4:4 Peeling off the newsprint.

Plate 16 Indonesian woman using a tjanting in a Jakarta workshop. Java (Kate Dean and Sally Coombes).

Plate 17 Three late 19th century batiks from Indonesia (Charles Beving Collection).

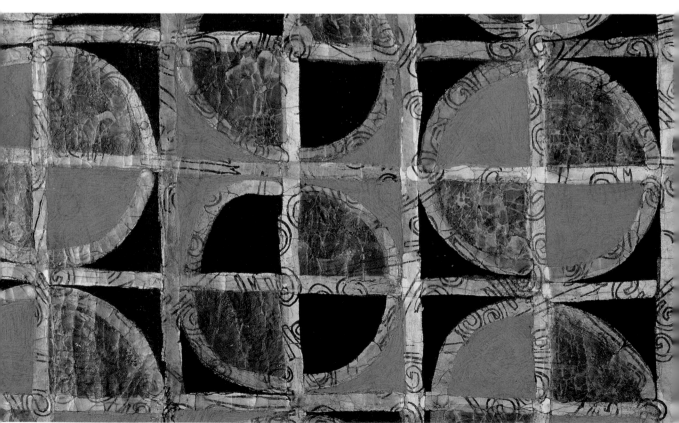

Plates 18 and 19 Wax resist wall hangings by Rushton Aust. Direct waxing and painting, combined with screen printing in *Plate 19*.

Plate 20 Batik kite by Steve Brockett. Steve stretches cotton fabric over the frame of the kite and then mixes Bricoprint fabric dyes with white spirit binder to form a gel. This is painted directly onto the fabric, firstly as an overall spray, then with brush strokes – the whole picture developing like a watercolour painting. As the kite panels are often bowed, it is impossible to fix the dyes with a hot iron – Steve uses a hot-air paint stripper.

Plate 21 Detail of batik dragonfly by Pat Hodson. Pat uses tjantings with a fine spout to produce finely drawn motifs such as flowers, landscapes and insects. She works mostly on silk and her scarves, screens and panels come from ideas developed in drawings.

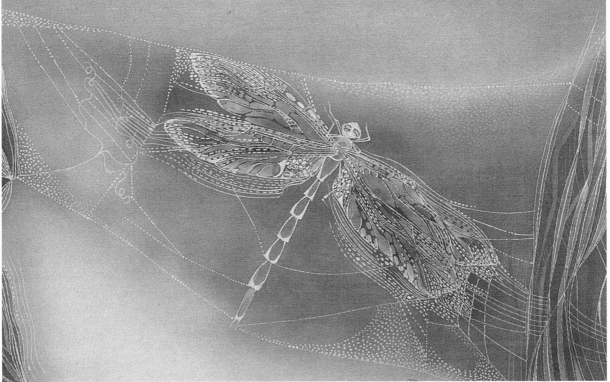

Plate 22 Batik wall hanging by Noel Dyrenforth.

remove the remaining wax and is in fact the traditional method of removing wax. It is important that your colours are fast when using this method, otherwise the colours will bleed. Lift fabric out of water using a pair of washing tongs as the fabric will be extremely hot. Avoid putting silk fabric in boiling water as this will cause it to shrivel. Use warm water for silk. Wax can be saved and re-used from the water you have just used. Allow the water to cool. The wax will float to the surface. Lift the wax out using a spoon or palette knife. Dry the wax out. It is ready to be re-used.

Avoid putting wax water down the sink as this will block the drains.

Modern dry cleaning methods can remove wax completely.

Gutta

The alternative to using wax as resist is to use a substance called gutta.

Gutta is a gum which you can buy in a plastic pipette. You pierce the pointed top on it with a pin and then sharpen to allow the gutta to flow onto the fabric in a thin continuous line. Special metal nibs can be bought which regulate the thickness of gutta line. When the gutta lines have dried on the fabric paint the areas without gutta with dye as in wax resist. Gutta can be bought colourless, black, silver or gold.

The advantages of using gutta is that it is easy and safe to use and is very portable. The pipette is much less liable to drip than a tjanting or a brush. The gutta flows slowly so you do not have to think so fast.

The disadvantages are that it is a gum therefore it tends to thicken in time especially in a warm atmosphere and therefore has to be diluted with white spirit. In general it does not run quite so smoothly as wax and is therefore less spontaneous. You cannot really use it with a brush and it does not produce the random marks which are characteristic of the wax resist process.

There is now available a large range of coloured and metallic resist mediums similar to gutta, sold in various sizes with their own applicator. These products not only act as a resist but can also enhance the design.

Resist dye painting

Many modern artists these days enjoy the versatility of using wax or gutta as a resist and directly painting on to the fabric with dyes (*Plates 18* and *19*). The advantage of this particular method is that you can create an infinite variety of colours and designs. By combining dyes and painting directly onto the fabric, dip dyeing the whole fabric can be avoided each time a new colour is required, yet the basic character of resist dyeing can be maintained. To achieve a crackle effect paint all the main areas of the design first and finish by painting the whole surface in wax to create a crackled effect (see page 79). This will give the effect of a true batik fabric, still retaining the freshness of painted fabric.

The painting technique very much resembles watercolour painting. Colours can be painted on top of each other to create another colour. They can be diluted to the required shade with water or a dilutant. The method for dye painting is as follows;

1 Many of the liquid dyes that can be bought for painting on fabric work equally well on silk, cotton or polyesters so they are extremely

versatile. They need to be fixed with a warm or hot iron, depending on the fabric you are using. In *Plates 18* and *19* the artist Rushton Aust has used a combination of direct waxing and painting to build up his abstract patterns. These wax paintings have wax left on them to add a textual or sculptural three dimensional effect to the work.

2 Draw the design on your fabric with a soft pencil or charcoal or alternatively place the fabric over a drawing of the design and tape to a flat surface. If you are stretching the fabric make sure it is evenly stretched so that the grain will not become distorted. This is particularly important in this method as the dye will collect in any dips in the fabric and will therefore not stain the fabric evenly if it is not properly stretched. The best way to stretch the fabric is to work from the centre, working outwards to the corners of the frame.

3 The next stage is to draw the design onto the fabric with hot wax using a tjanting. Remember when using a white fabric the lines you make with the tjanting will remain white. Therefore it may be more suitable to paint in areas of the design in the lighter shades first, and then wax over the other parts of the design.

4 If you want the dyes to blend with each other and give a soft watercolour effect saturate the fabric first with water and merely drop in the colour and the colour will flow rapidly across the fabric. This works particularly well with fine materials such as silk or thin polyester. Tones of any colour can be made using the same method as mixing watercolours, by simply diluting the colour with water. It is helpful to collect lots of yoghurt pots as they can be used to make up lots of different shades.

5 To produce a uniform tone between the areas of resist then use an appropriate sized brush (sable are very good for this). Dip the brush into the dye then paint on the dye. There is usually no need to paint right up to the resist lines as the dye will travel over the taut fabric. If you paint too close to the line there is a danger that the dye might seep over the line into another area.

6 To create more richness in a design wait until the original painted areas have dried. Then wax over them again to build up more dye on top. This can be done several times so that when the wax is removed by ironing it will reveal all the various tones contained by the waxed lines and areas.

7 Large areas can be dyed in the bath. Alternatively they can be painted directly using a large decorator's brush or sponge. It is important to flood the colour on quickly and evenly.

Transfer dyeing

Transfer dyeing is painting of a design on paper and then the printing it onto fabric. The design is transferred by ironing. It is easier to paint directly onto paper and to iron the paper onto fabric than to stretch the fabric over a frame. The fabric most suitable for this process will be synthetic or a blend of synthetic and natural fabric such as polyester cotton. It is possible to print on natural fabrics with this process but generally the results are disappointing. It is worth experimenting with different fabrics as the results vary enormously – on thinner fabrics the image tends to be brighter and you can often get two prints from one design. It is possible to buy transfer crayons at many department stores and specialist art suppliers. They are very easy for children to handle but they must be used with care as any unwanted specks of crayon left on the design will print. Crayons can also be used in combination with the transfer dyes as it is easier to get a good line with a crayon than with a paintbrush dipped in dye.

The dyes used for transfer dyeing come in small jars and are dilutable with water. It is essential to do a test piece on the fabric that is being used for a project because the colour effect varies according to the type of fabric that is used. The dyes can be used the same way as watercolours; subtle effects can be obtained if the paper is dampened first with plenty of water and small quantities of dye then dropped into the damp areas.

There are also many ways to apply these dyes. They can be sprayed onto the paper with a mouthspray or an airbrush, or spattered with a tooth-brush. A stencil or mask, such as a paper doyley, can be placed between the paper and the fabric so that colour will not be transferred where the doyley has been placed.

The iron is best used to press rather than to slide – you need to build up heat through the paper to transfer the dye. Indeed, the iron must be as hot as the fabric will stand. It is usually a good idea to tape the paper down at the corners with masking tape so that paper does not move with the use of the iron – although double images can be achieved in this way.

Batik projects

Batik can be used to make clothes – shirts, dresses, fashion accessories such as bags and scarves; soft furnishings – blinds, lampshades, screens, cushions, kites and dolls for children.

Wax resist shawl

The shawl featured (4:5) was decorated by wax resist rather than by the strict batik method. That is all the colours came from painting onto the cloth rather than from dipping the whole shawl into a dyebath.

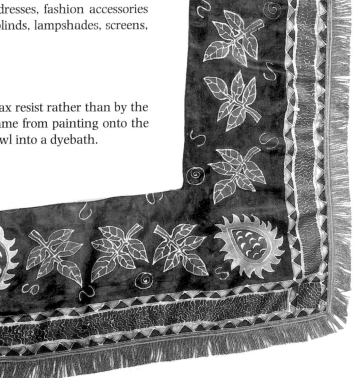

4:5 Painted shawl with a gold fringe.

Materials
1 m thin white silk satin
Deka dyes – gold, green, black
Electric tjanting
Paintbrushes no. 6
plus large decorator's brush
Batik wax
2 m tassel fringe trim

Method
1 Draw the design firmly with pencil onto a large sheet of paper measuring 1 m square.

2 Lay the piece of paper on a flat surface (a large board or table will do) and tape it down to the surface with masking tape or Sellotape.

3 Lay the silk fabric (cut 2 cm larger all round than the paper) over the design and tape this to the flat surface.

4 Heat the wax in the tjanting and trace over the lines round the border of the designs (4:6). These are the only lines which will stay white.

4:6 Following the lines of a drawn design with an electric tjanting.

5 Then make half a jam jarful of the diluted first dye (green in this case).

6 Remove the silk from the paper and stretch it over a suitable frame – see page 87. Attach with silk pins or masking tape to edges of the frame. When the silk is stretched paint the whole surface with dye. Leave this to dry.

7 Take off the silk, put back over the paper and attach with tape. Then trace with wax all the outlines of the leaves, the S motifs and other decorative motifs. These will remain a light green.

8 Next take the fabric off the paper and stretch it back on the frame. Paint on the second dye (gold) (*4:7*) inside the triangular shapes on the border, the leaves and the large motifs, and in between the squiggly lines round the border. Gold is also painted on the edge of the large motif and as stripes along the edge of the border.

4:7 Painting on Deka dye.

9 The final stage is to apply black over the background and in the remaining triangles of the border.

10 When the fabric is dry iron off the wax between several sheets of newsprint or old newspaper. Then iron over the whole surface to fix the Deka dyes see page 59 (*4:8*). Follow the instructions for fixing the dye. Turn in a 1 cm seam all round the shawl and sew on the fringe with matching thread.

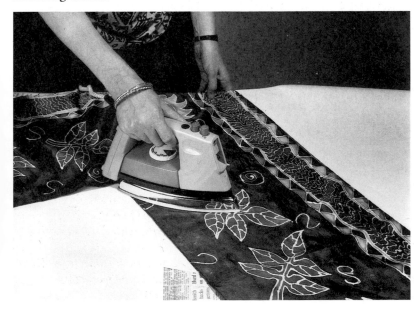

4:8 Fixing Deka dye with a hot iron.

Batik shirt

The shirt illustrated in *4:9* uses traditional batik technique. It is predominantly dark purple with a geometrically patterned border along the bottom, sleeves and collar. The patterned border consists of many colours. These are built up with yellow, red and blue dyes, in this order, dyeing and waxing being repeated to achieve many shades.

Materials
To make the shirt
Shirt pattern
Dressmaker's paper
3 m white cotton lawn
50 cm medium iron-on vilene for the collar and front facings
6 shirt buttons
Machine thread
Pins
Needles
Dressmaker's scissors

4:9 Completed batik shirt by Mary Spyrou.

For batik
Tailor's chalk
Silk pins
Photographic tray or shallow bath
Washing tongs
Tjantings – small, medium, large
Beeswax or a mixture of beeswax and paraffin wax
Variety of painting brushes
Batik frame
Charcoal pencil or sticks
Electric ring or cooker
3 × 25 g containers of Procion dye: yellow, red, and blue

Method
  1 Wash fabric to remove dirt, grease and finish (see page 53).
  2 Make any necessary adjustments to shirt pattern.
  3 Lay out pattern pieces on the fabric following the instructions
provided. Remember to place pieces along the grain.
  4 Pin pieces in place. Cut out fabric marking notches. Make tailor's
tacks where necessary.
  5 Tape cartoon of geometric design to table (*4:10*). Place a main shirt
piece over the design cartoon positioning 6 cm from the bottom edge of
the shirt. Allow 4 cm for the hem. Trace design with a charcoal pencil or
stick (*4:11*). Repeat this stage with all the pieces except the sleeves
where only the narrowest part of the design is used – from the edge of
the hexagon to the first solid line of colour.

4:10 Design in paper collage for use on the shirt.   *4:11* Drawing design onto stretched fabric.

  6 Stretch a shirt piece on the batik frame, securing in place with silk
pins. The size of the frame can be adjusted to a number of sizes to
accommodate the size of your fabric.
  7 Heat the wax in a batik pot (see page 77).

8 Take a medium size tjanting and carefully draw over the lines (*4:12*). This will eventually create a white outline (the colour of the fabric). To avoid getting any drips on the fabric, either hold a piece of paper or card under the tjanting to catch the drips as you follow the lines, or quickly wipe the tjanting with a piece of rag as you take it from the wax pot. Avoid overfilling the tjanting with wax.

4:12 First waxing.

9 Allow the wax to dry and cool properly on the fabric before you apply the first colour. Use a light colour for the first dip (*4:13*). In this case yellow is used. Pour dye into a shallow bath such as a photographic tray which is light and easy to agitate. Washing tongs are useful for moving the batik pieces gently around, enabling the dye to penetrate evenly. All the pieces can be dyed together, though you may prefer to do a few at a time. Be careful not to let the dye exhaust itself. A dyebath is usually active for approximately two hours.

10 After the first dyeing (*4:14*) rinse pieces carefully in cold water. Remove excess water by placing the batik pieces between paper. Allow to dry in a well ventilated room or hang on a washing line from one corner, this will prevent any dye streaking.

11 When the shirt pieces are dry stretch again on the batik frame. You may need to touch up any lines that have lost wax during the first dyeing.

12 Take a medium size brush and wax in the geometric shapes. This will preserve areas of yellow fabric to form the yellow shapes of the patterned border.

13 Make up a red dye bath (see page 56). Dip the batik pieces as before, repeating stages 9–10 twice, to create different shades of red which can be achieved by varying the length of time you dip for.

14 Repeat the waxing process and dye blue. Continue until you feel you have the desired number of colours from yellow, red and blue.

4:13 First dyeing.

4:14 Fabric after first dyeing to show waxed and unwaxed areas.

15 Wax the patterned border completely. Crackle the patterned border (*4:15*) and dip in a dyebath of dark colour, such as navy or black. (Basically use any colour providing it is darker than the last colour used, to create a contrast between the crackle and the main pattern) (*4:16*).

16 There are a number of ways you can remove the wax (see page 80 for instructions) (*4:3* and *4:4*).

17 To make the shirt firstly ensure all pieces are well ironed. Follow the pattern instructions provided.

4:15 Fabric crumpled in order to crack the wax.

4:16 Fabric flattened again and redyed.

Batik jacket

Jap silk (1 m) was used to make the batik jacket seen below. The collar ruffle and sleeve ruffles and the cone-shaped pieces appliquéed onto the body of the jacket were all cut from white mediumweight silk which had been entirely painted in wax and crackled by hand and then dipped in a dyebath which matched the colour of the fabric for the jacket.

Method

1 The white jap silk is first washed, dried, ironed and stretched over a frame.

2 Use a pencil or marker pen to mark off a strip of 10 cm × 1 m – this is for the neck ruffle. Mark another strip of 10 cm × 1 m. This is for the two sleeve ruffles. The rest of the fabric when dyed can be cut up for the appliqué triangles.

3 Wax the entire area except for a strip down the long edge of each long strip measuring 1 cm wide – this is to give a very narrow border of colour to the neck and sleeve ruffles as a contrast edging to the crackled fabric. Wax evenly and check the back to make sure there are no gaps in the wax surface.

4 Take the fabric off the frame, crumple evenly in your hands and submerge in the dyebath.

5 When the fabric has absorbed the dye (see batik instructions page 80), iron between sheets of old newspaper to remove wax. You will find that unless you have the waxed fabric dry cleaned, the wax will not come out completely. This can be used to some advantage for if the silk is slightly stiffer it can be easier to sew and will stand up better as ruffles.

6 Cut out the strips and use a template to cut out triangular pieces for the appliqué.

7 Make the strips for the ruffles using the tucking technique (described on page 102) and the sewing on of the appliqué pieces is done by machine as described on page 38.

See *2:15*.

Survey

Indonesia

Traditionally, Indonesian textiles (*Plate 17*) served many functions. They were used for barter and even as a form of currency in times of hardship. They were also used as talismans to ward off and cure illness. Batiks had important ritual significance, as in initiation ceremonies, and were an important inheritance. They were worn to identify rank and profession, often being worn in combination with a weapon in the display of regalia. Textiles were regarded as symbolically female, relating to the sexual division of labour. The women were responsible for the harvesting of the silk and cotton and for the tjanting designs while men did the weaving and dyeing.

Traditionally indigenous natural dyes were used. The most popular colours were soga brown and indigo blue. Also turkey red (morinda) and yellow (curcuma). The soga brown is almost unique to Indonesia, rarely found anywhere else. The soga brown is extracted from bark which is chopped and soaked in a mordant, and comes in a variety of shades from reddish to dark brown. Often indigo dyed fabric is repeatedly overdyed with soga brown to get black. Nowadays with the widespread use of synthetic dyes an unlimited variety of colours can be achieved and traditional dyeing methods are extremely rare. Most dyeing is now done in factories.

4:17 Selection of batik examples (tjanting techniques).

With the increasing demand for export, traditional hand drawn fabrics known as tulis have been largely replaced by the tjap printed batiks, to speed up production. The tjap was introduced to Java from Madras in 1850 where it had been in use since the fifteenth century. Tjaps are used by men and the tjanting by women.

Batiks are worn as many styles of dress (*Plate 16*). The most commonly worn batik by both men and women is the sarong, a square or rectangular cloth which is stitched up to form a wide tube. This can be easily stepped into, drawn up and folded round the hips, then either knotted or belted round the waist. The Sarong is a cool form of skirt and ideal for the humid climate of Indonesia. Sarongs can be seen worn with Western shirts and blouses. Other varieties of everyday dress include the ikat or kain kapala worn by both men and women – by men as a turban. A slendang or kemben is a narrow strip of cloth worn as a sash or breast cloth, or sometimes tied as a sling to carry a baby or baskets of food.

Worn as a more formal style of dress by men is the kain pandjang or bebed. A ceremonial batik is the dodot, a large garment of about three and a half by two metres. This is worn by both men and women and was traditionally worn by the courts only. Nowadays it is worn at weddings. Dodots tend to come in two designs either with a large lozenge shaped centre within a highly decorative border or an overall design. Dodots are usually worn with a train of ikat weave called a patola. Batiks used for festival occasions were sometimes decorated with gold leaf. These are called pradas.

A very ingenious batik design is one called a 'pagi-sore' which literally translated, means morning and evening. It carries two batik designs on one garment, allowing the wearer to reveal one design in the morning and another in the evening.

Numerous batik designs display a great variety of imagery which is often symbolic, inspired by the flora and fauna of the islands, heraldry and the traditional cloud motif, snakes and phoenix brought by the Chinese who settled in the north of Java. The figures of the puppet theatre known as wayang form perhaps the oldest batik design dating back to A.D. 1000. Humans appeared in a very stylised form as any figurative or animal representation was forbidden by the Koran, and acted out moral tales, religious stories and also comedy. There were certain designs known as forbidden designs. These were reserved for the courts and included a design called parang – a spiralling form laid out along diagonal lines traditionally containing such motifs as the swastika, the symbol of good luck and peace. Another design is the 'semen', a naturalistic representation of sprouting leaves, plants, flowers and curling tendrils. The kawung motif has arrangements of ovals and ellipses grouped in fours, believed to be of Persian origin reminiscent of heraldic symbols. Finally tjeplok consists of repeated natural forms in patterns of circles and squares.

The designs are either waxed from memory if the craftsperson is particularly skilled or taken from a drawn pattern. It was said in the past that women often prepared themselves for drawing with the tjanting by reaching a meditative state. The main batik areas are in central and northern Java at Pankalongan, Cheribon, Jogjakarta and Surakarta. Some modern

4:18 Indonesian tjanting work.

batiks are illustrated in *4:2*.

Paste resist is also practised in Indonesia amongst the Toraja peoples of the Central Celebes who use wooden bamboo stamps to decorate the cloth that is used for shrouds.

Indo-China

The Meo people live in the hills between south-west China and northern Thailand. The women practise fine wax drawing with an iron pen on linen, producing designs from memory. They consist of fine geometric patterns which are dyed indigo. Appliqué motifs of black and white cotton are added and embroidered with yellow and red cross stitch. The decorated fabric is then made into finely pleated skirts.

5 Other decorative techniques with fabric

Introduction

This chapter is devoted to the decorative techniques which apply largely to clothing. These techniques have a long history in many cultures. In the Western Europe of the late 19th century women's costume was particularly elaborate, with a prevalence of braids, fringes, ribbons, ruchings, bows, scallops and flounces. Dresses of this period were long, very close fitting to reveal the form of the body in the front and extended to form the bustle at the back. Jacket bodices with peplums became popular and often the front of the dress was left open to show the lace frilled chemisette. It became fashionable in the 1870s to use two or more different materials to make up dresses. The popularity of different colours and textures of materials continued during 1880s as well as the heavy decoration particularly of the train of the bustle, skirts of dresses which were often draped, gathered or set into pleats. Often the draped skirts were controlled by tie catching. In the mid 1880s the trains became longer and were decorated by a profusion of ribbons, bows, lace falls, ruffles and accordion pleating. By the 1890s the decoration had become simpler though edgings, flat braids and frogging were still popular but by now decoration was mainly featured on the bodice of the dress. These bodice decorations of bows, lace ribbons, tucks and pleatings became more dramatic with the influence of Art Nouveau.

In some respects current dress worn by women from Pakistan and parts of northern India reminds us of decoration that has been missing from Western dress since the early days of this century. Whilst fashion in Europe has been more subject to extremes of cut, hem length, amounts of fabric used, etc., there has been less of an emphasis on decoration though recently there has been a redeveloped interest in the manipulation of fabric, e.g. ruching and gathering.

Although the basic shape of a woman's shalwar kameez (trousers and tunic) worn in Britain, northern India and Pakistan does not vary a great deal, fashion plays quite a big part in the kind of decorative techniques which are applied. Shalwar kameez are worn by both the Muslims of Pakistan and the Hindus and Sikhs of East Punjab in India. Although there are differences of style and colour, the symbolic meaning is the same for all Punjabis. Older women from Kashmir often wear the Kashmiri style where the kameez is rather long and often has a definite waistline and the shalwar has a stiff deep cuff at the ankle. The scarf which is traditionally worn with the shalwar kameez to cover a woman's hair (called a dupatta in

Pakistan and a chunni in India) can hang loosely round the neck or be draped round the head and shoulders.

Although clothes are often imported, many women in Britain are very skilled at making and designing their own shalwar kameez. They can be made up in a plain style but many women favour such decorative techniques as ruching, faggoting, rouleaux, piping, quilting and binding, and often incorporate matching or contrasting buttons, frills, etc. Individual dressmaker's preferences are shown in the types and combinations of decorative feature used; some may be traditional and some influenced by what is currently popular in the fashions of the adopted country. This all develops as an interesting fusion of style.

Techniques

Rouleau work

Rouleau work is a popular decoration for the neckline of shalwar kameez (5:1 and 5:2). Rouleau tubes consist of bias-cut strips of fabric which are seamed together and turned inside out. For very fine tubing, use thin silky polyester. Because rouleaux are cut on the bias they can then be formed into interesting designs. They are often linked together with faggoting which is a way of joining these pieces of rouleau by a simple twisted stitch (5:3).

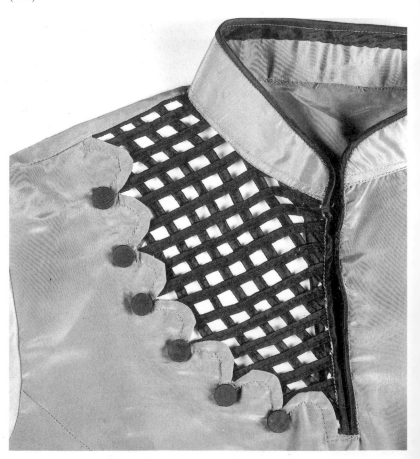

5:1 Ochre silk dress with dark brown criss-crossed flat rouleaux and matching covered buttons by Shahnaz Aslam.

Plate 23 Details of ruched velvet evening dresses by Sue Jones

Plate 24 Decorative panel by Margo
Singer. Spray-dyed and pin tucked.

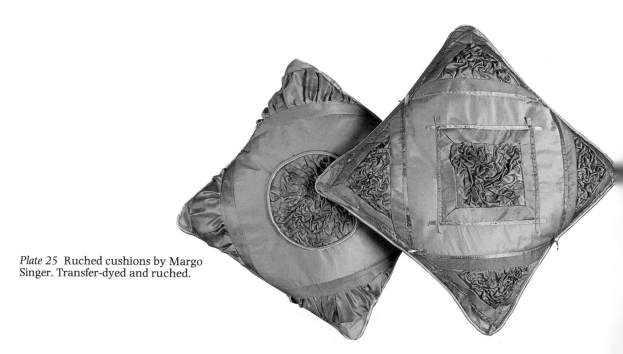

Plate 25 Ruched cushions by Margo
Singer. Transfer-dyed and ruched.

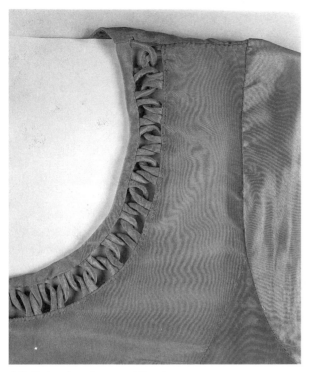

5:2 Twisted rouleau neckline in pale blue silk by Shahnaz Aslam.

5:3 Part of a bodice by Shahnaz Aslam. Twisted tucks on the shoulder with smocking and faggoting at the front neck edge.

Making rouleau tubes

The finished width of the tubing can vary from 5 mm to 1 cm according to the effect that is required.

1 Cut several strips of fabric on the cross approx 3 cm wide. Join as for bias binding (page 108).

2 Fold the strips lengthwise with the right sides inside and machine stitch approximately 1 cm from the edge.

3 Trim the raw edges.

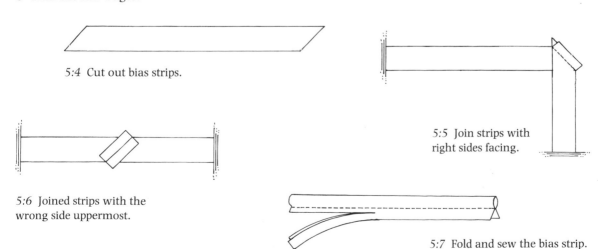

5:4 Cut out bias strips.

5:5 Join strips with right sides facing.

5:6 Joined strips with the wrong side uppermost.

5:7 Fold and sew the bias strip.

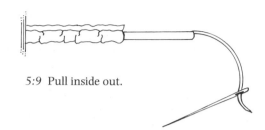

5:8 Insert a bodkin attached to one end of the strip.

5:9 Pull inside out.

4 Use a safety pin or a bodkin, to turn the strip inside out. If using a safety pin insert this near the open end through just one of the two layers. If using a bodkin, thread it and secure the thread to the open end by stitching it.

5 Draw the bodkin or pin through the entire length of the tube so that the fabric is turned to its right side.

6 The tube can be ironed flat at this stage or it can be left unpressed if a softer appearance is desired.

Using rouleaux as decoration

1 Decide where the rouleau is wanted on a piece of decorative work, a garment or a piece of soft furnishing. Draw the design on some thin paper (pattern paper or typing paper is fine). Remember to indicate on the design the width of the rouleau tubing as this will affect the final look of the design.

2 Using the drawn design as the guideline, tack the rouleau strips in place onto the paper with a tacking thread in a contrasting colour so it is easy to take out.

3 When the design is finished the entire piece can be mounted on the garment. Use a matching thread to stitch the pieces of rouleau where they overlap or else when the paper is torn away the whole design will collapse. When this has been done, sew the design to the fabric and carefully tear away the backing paper.

When the design is in place you can decide where and if to use faggoting. This will reinforce the rouleau strips and will add to the decoration.

If a simpler and quicker method of rouleau work is desired and if the design of the rouleau strips is one which does not involve curves but is only a crisscross design or a woven design it is possible to make tubes from lengthwise strips of fabric. The design can be made in the same way on paper but it can be machined together through the centre of each rouleau strip rather than hand sewn. This is a fairly fast and simple method which can be done with straight lines.

Weaving with the rouleau tubes (5:1)

Interesting designs can be made by weaving rouleaux.

1 Decide on the area you want to cover with rouleaux – this can be a strip, a square or a circle. Whatever the shape of the finished piece start by arranging on a padded board (or the ironing board) the pieces of rouleau tubing you want to use as warp yarns (running downwards).

2 Pin these with ordinary dressmaker's pins to the board at the top and the bottom so that they are fairly tight. You can then weave the weft of

5:10 Flat machined rouleaux.

the rouleau tubes in and out between the warp rouleaux. You can make an interesting texture by using plain material and an even more interesting one by using patterned or dyed material as you can vary the design by deciding where to put each colour.

5:11 Woven rouleaux.

5:12 Neckline of twisted rouleaux in purple, blue and white floral polyester fabric by Shahnaz Aslam.

3 When the design is finished it is a good idea to secure the pieces with pins and tacking. Mount where desired and sew into place. Rouleau strips can also be twisted to achieve an interesting effect (see *5:2* and *5:12*).

Tied rouleaux

Tying rouleaux by stitching can give a very decorative appearance. This is achieved by stitching through the rouleau strips at intervals and fastening off. This can be done at regular or irregular intervals and with a matching or contrasting thread. It gives a bead-like appearance to the rouleaux.

Faggoting

Faggoting is a technique of using stitches to join pieces of fabric together. Faggoting stitches produce decorative seams and can be used on their own or with rouleaux to create rich designs and patterns. It is possible to use faggoting to join together most fabrics from silky weights to heavy woollens.

The variations of faggoting stitches are shown in *5:13* to *5:15*.

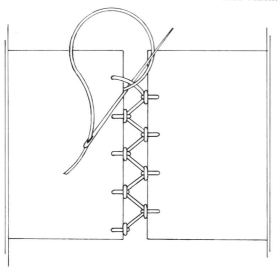

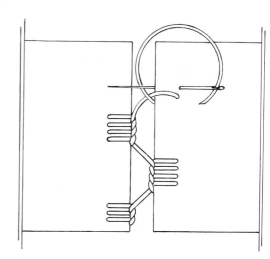

5:13 to 5:15 Faggoting.

5:14

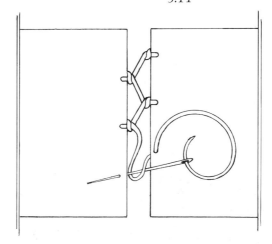

5:15

Ruching

Ruching was a popular technique used in the nineteenth century when it was widely used (*5:16*). It made a comeback in the 1930s in Britain and was used to more effect as it now was used to enhance the shape of a garment not just as an embellishment.

Again it is a technique to be found decorating the necklines or shoulders or sleeves of shalwar kameez.

It is also known as gathered quilting and is often used in making cushions particularly in velvet which looks especially luxurious when ruched (*Plate 23*). It also gives a very luscious effect on satins of different weights (*Plate 25*).

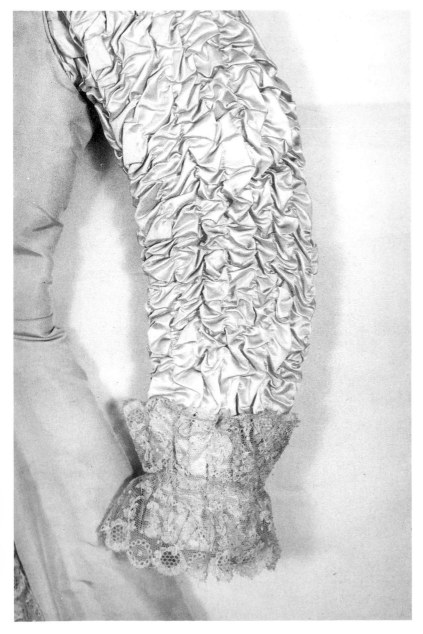

5:16 Detail of ruched sleeve from the 1880s (Platt Hall Museum).

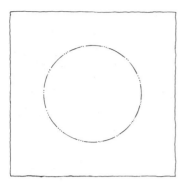

5:17 to 5:20 Ruching.

5:18

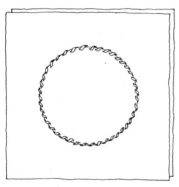

5:19

5:20

Materials

For this you need two layers of fabric, one which is fairly stable (calico or medium weight cotton is good for this) and a thinner fabric which is to be ruched.

Method

1 Mark the shape of the area to be covered with ruching; this can be any shape regular or irregular (*5:17*). From the lightweight fabric cut a similar shape but approximately twice the size. Mark a hem on the wrong side.

2 Sew a line of running stitch right round the edge and draw this thread up to make the edges the same length as those of the shape required (*5:18*).

3 Place this over the desired shape and sew into place. This will give you a loose bag and this can be gathered onto the background in any way you like (*5:19*).

4 Stitch at intervals through this top fabric onto background and this will create an interesting surface texture. This can be combined with beads, sequins or small interesting embroidery stitches if you wish to add to the decorative effect.

Ruched strips

This technique featured quite commonly in the nineteenth century to form long bands on the trains or sides of dresses and is a simple and effective way of creating interest on plain garments.

Materials

Soft material such as silk, polyester and lawn is best used here.

Method

To make a strip of ruched fabric you have first to decide where you want to position it and to measure the length of the flat piece of fabric you are attaching it to. Allow approximately one and a half to two times the length when cutting the fabric to ruch. Run two rows of machine stitching down each long end of the strip to be gathered. Remember to use stitch length 4 and a loose tension so that the threads can gather the material. You can use hand gathering if you prefer but this is much slower. The stitching lines should be with the normal 1.5 cm seam allowance. Gather these up to make the ruched fabric fit the flat fabric, pin in place, tack and then sew together. If you want the strip to curve tighten up one side more than the other.

Tucks

Tucks and pleats are often used as decoration on a particular section of clothing – often at the centre front or on the sleeves. They can also be used as decoration on smaller areas such as the collar or a pocket.

Tucks are the more decorative of the two – they can be made vertically or horizontally and are usually stitched from one end to the other whereas pleats (pressed or unpressed) are left open for at least part of their length.

Tucks take up very little extra fabric if they are sewn close to the fold but you will have to allow a little extra when calculating the amount of material to be used. The fabrics which are best for tucking are soft ones: silks, crepes, soft woollens and cottons, and silky polyesters.

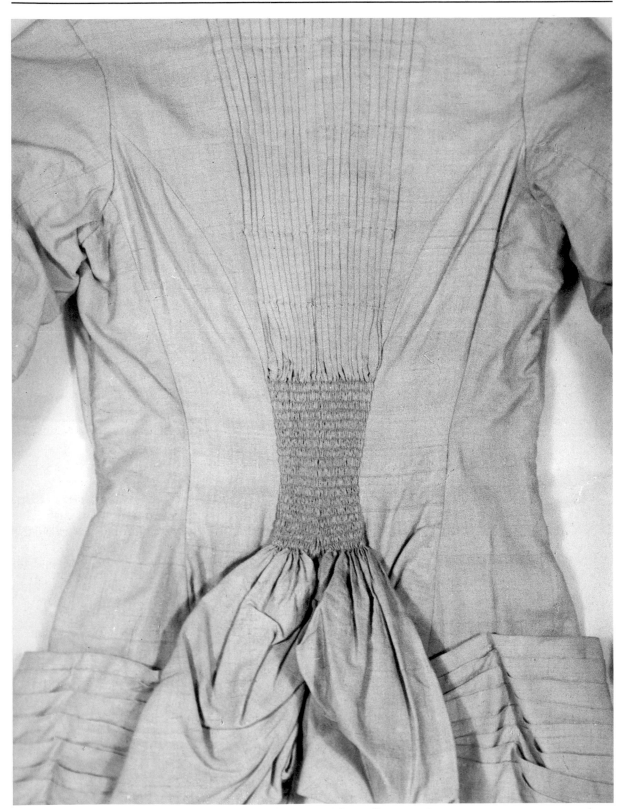

5:21 The back of an 1880s' dress with tucking and gathering (Platt Hall Museum).

It will help to make these tucks if you attach a quilting foot to your sewing machine so that you can line up the tucks as you go along. Most machines have a special quilting foot as one of their accessories. It is a piece of shaped metal which is lowered with the presser foot onto the fabric and acts as a visual guide. It is also a useful attachment as a seam guide: when you want to make seams of a different size, you adjust the quilting foot accordingly.

Iron or crease a fold where you want the first tuck to be and stitch along the fold. Tucks are usually stitched about 3 mm from the fold but you can stitch anywhere you think appropriate – the tucks seen in *Plate 24* – are stitched 5 mm from the edge. To ensure evenness of tucks you must mark their position on the fabric unless you are doing a free piece of work. Tucks can lie in the same direction or you can change their direction by stitching across them. Tucks can be spaced evenly or they can be positioned very close together in groups.

Pintucks

If you want tucks that do not lie flat, make the tucks as narrow as possible and press them with a soft cloth from the wrong side so that they stand up.

An interesting development of this technique which produces an attractive effect with less fabric is a stitch made on a sewing machine with the raised seam presser foot and the double needle. The foot attachment has a groove on the underside which matches a ridge in the accompanying plate that fits over the feed teeth. This forces the fabric up into a little ridge (*Plate 24*). The double needle can be bought with different spacings from a sewing machine shop. It can be threaded with two threads of the same colour or two contrasting threads to give more effect. The sewing holds the ridge in place.

Do not use too small a stitch for this may stiffen the tucks and they will not lie well. Tucks are usually stitched in the same colour thread as the fabric but you can experiment with contrasting threads. Crossed tucks look especially attractive but be careful if you want to sew across the grain diagonally as this can distort the fabric. When you are stitching a group of tucks always sew them in the same direction if you want to avoid distorting the fabric.

Shell edging

This is another form of tucking which can look attractive on hems.

Frills

Frills have been used on clothing for centuries. They can be added to almost anywhere on a garment to make it more decorative and luxurious. A frill is basically a strip of fabric, normally cut on the straight grain, gathered or pleated and then stitched onto a garment. Generally a frill should be at least one and a half times the width of the fabric it is being joined to. This depends on the fabric used for the frill and if it is very lightweight more material can be put into it. It is possible to make frills out of almost any fabric from silk chiffon to soft leather.

The method for making a frill is as follows:

Hem one long edge while the strip of fabric is still flat. Run two parallel lines of stitching along the opposite edge either by hand or machine. The

5:22 Opposite: Victorian lady in a ruched and pleated dress of the 1880s (Platt Hall Museum).

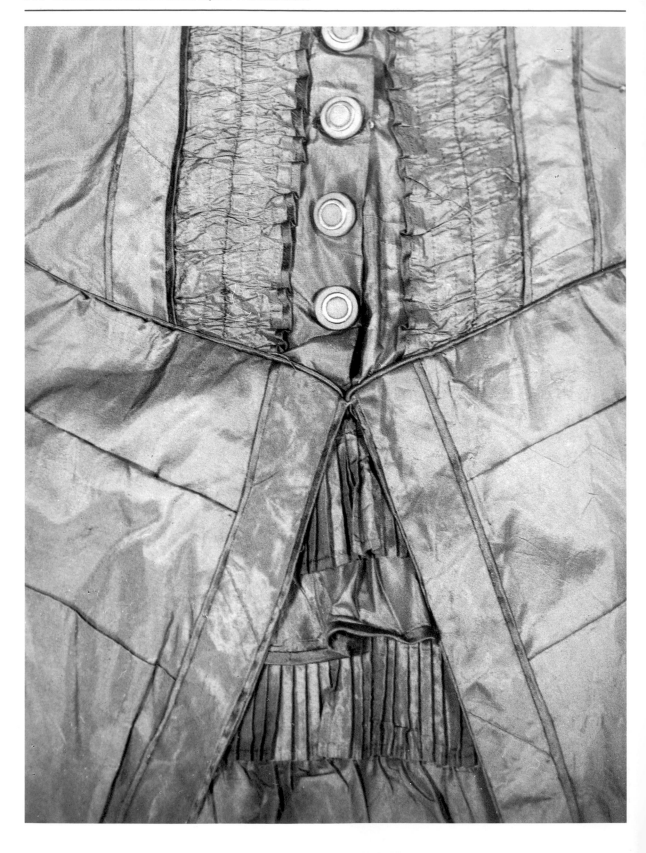

rest of the procedure is similar to that described for ruching, on page 101. If you are making a frill for the entire hem of a garment, stitch all the strips of fabric together to make the frill, then mark both the frill and the hem into quarters before pinning, tacking and sewing together.

An alternative frill to stitch onto the edge of a garment has both long edges hemmed before it is gathered and laid on top of the unfinished edge of the garment (on the right side). Then pin, tack and top-stitch through the frill onto the fabric. You need to leave about 2 or 3 cm on the head of the frill to make it look attractive. This method of making a frill was very popular with Victorian dressmakers and features on the hem of the dress (5:22).

You can finish the edges of this type of frill in various ways by zigzagging the edge or using a decorative machine embroidery stitch on the edge or finishing the edge with bias binding.

Instead of fabric, ribbons can be used for frills – the advantage of these is that they already have finished edges on each side and so are relatively quick to gather up and attach to a garment. They can, of course, also be applied flat onto the garment for decoration or made into bows and scattered about. They can be used very effectively to catch up gathered and flounced material. This was popular on Victorian dresses.

Flounces

A flounce has something of the appearance of a frill but it is a strip of fabric cut on the bias which is attached to the garment flat, without being gathered. Flounces were popular in the Victorian era and also in the 1920s and 1930s when they were used on necklines and skirts managing to soften the rather austere lines of the dresses.

The materials which work best for flounces are obviously soft ones: cotton, crepe, silk and wool: plain fabrics work better on the whole than patterned ones as the right and wrong side of the fabric look the same and both sides of a flounce will often show.

There are many ways of making flounces. The most simple is to attach a piece of square material by its point to a neckline and to let it hang freely. Fullness in a flounce is made by cutting curved bands of fabric and sewing them to parts of a garment, usually the neckline or sleeve wrist. If you use circles of fabric to cut flounces from, you will discover that you can vary the amount of fullness, the smallest circle giving you the maximum fullness. Neck ruffles can be made from more than one layer of flounces and several circles can be joined to make more flounces.

Cut a paper pattern for the part of the garment where you want to add a flounce. If you want a 4 panelled skirt with flounces, for example, first make a paper pattern for your 4 panels. Draw a line up the middle of each panel and cut along the line from the bottom to within 1 cm of the top (but add a seam allowance). Splay out the pattern as wide as you wish the flounce to be and then make another wider paper pattern incorporating the flounce. Use this new pattern to cut out your fabric.

Bias binding

One of the decorative techniques which finishes a garment well is the technique of binding and piping the edges of garments and soft furnishings. This is illustrated (5:23) in the 1880s and also features on one of

5:23 Opposite: detail of ruching, tucking, binding and piping from the 1880s (Platt Hall Museum).

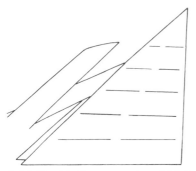

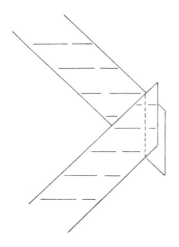

5:24 Bias binding: cut strips of fabric on the bias.

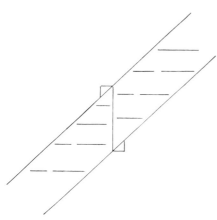

5:25 Join strips together with the right sides facing.

5:26 The joined strips with the right side uppermost.

the kameez made by Shahnaz (5:1 and 5:27).

Materials
Bias binding can be bought from haberdashery departments in most big stores or in specialist dress material shops. It comes in cotton or polyester satin in two widths, 2.5 cm and 1.5 cm wide.

Bias binding can also be made from strips of material cut on the bias from fabric that matches or contrasts with the article to be bound (5:24).

Method
This is done by finding the grain of the fabric and cutting strips along the bias to the width that you require. To join the bias strips end to end to make a longer strip, cut the end of each bias strip on the straight grain (this should give you a slant in the same direction on each end) and then, with right sides together, machine the strips together with a 5 mm seam (5:25). Press open and trim off any pieces that protrude. The finished piece of bias binding will look like 5:26.

Method of binding edges
To bind a straight edge of fabric, pin the raw edge of the bias strip to the edge of the fabric, right sides facing each other, tack and stitch on the machine along the fold line on commercial bias binding. The bias binding is then turned over the edge and the second fold tacked down. (In the case of bias binding that you have made, turn in the raw edge before tacking). Then machine from the right side or sew by hand (hemstitch) on the wrong side. If you are binding a curved seam you will have to stretch the binding on the outer edge and ease the binding on the inner edge when tacking. When stitching a curve it is usually easier to slipstitch on the wrong side as this is difficult to sew by machine.

5:27 Smocked green silk dress edged with black bias binding by Shahnaz Aslam.

Binding corners

The method for making an attractive and neat mitred corner is as follows: with right sides together place the edge of the bias binding 2 mm less than half the binding width from the edge, tack then machine 2 mm from the edge to the corner, backstitch by machine for a couple of stitches. Then fold the binding at the corner diagonally so that it continues at 90° to the first edge. Tack, then machine sew. Fold the binding to the wrong side to form a mitre at the corner. Hem by hand.

Often the front of a dress with a V neck needs binding and the following method will make a neat finish. Stay stitch for about 3 cm on either side of the point of the V.

Piping

Piping consists of piping cord which is stranded cotton, with a strip of homemade or purchased bias binding which is cut approximately 2–4 cm wide depending on the thickness of piping cord. The strip is folded over the cord enclosing it and sewn by machine as close as possible to the cord using the zipper or piping foot on your machine. To attach to the edge of a cushion it is sandwiched between 2 layers of fabric (right sides together) then stitched through the 3 layers. If the corners are to be curved remember to clip all 3 layers. Piping can be used as edging or a decorative feature inserted between a seam on a garment. Examples of piping can be found on page 115, the ruched cushion, and page 68, the tie and dye cushion.

Shirring

Another way of gathering fabric is shirring which consists of several rows of gathering. This technique is traditionally applied to waists and cuffs and is quite popular on the legs of trousers. It can look decorative on other parts of garments, too, and is a way of controlling fullness. Shirring can be used for a whole bodice of an evening dress or as a decorative feature at the top of the sleeves or on the pockets. Shirring is usually carried out on a sewing machine with elastic thread on the bobbin and ordinary sewing thread on top of the machine.

Method

If you are making rows of shirring below an edge such as a hem or a cuff, finish the edge first as it is too difficult afterwards. Wind elastic thread (bought at most haberdashers) onto the bobbin by hand without stretching it. Set the machine tension to normal or with longer stitches for tighter shirring and sew rows of stitching from 10 mm to 25 mm apart leaving thread at each end of each row. Check the width of the piece of shirring and if this is not the right width you can pull or adjust the threads to make it the required size. Bring all the top sewing threads to the wrong side of the fabric and knot with the elastic ends.

Buttons

Apart from the very decorative buttons you can now buy in most stores for a really individual garment you can make your own very simply. Most haberdashery shops sell self cover buttons or button covering kits which

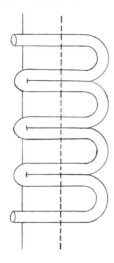

5:28 Button loops made from rouleaux.

come with full instructions on the back of the packet. They come in a wide variety of sizes.

If you are going to the trouble of making buttons of matching or coordinating fabric then it is worthwhile making corded button loops to match. These look very decorative down the back of a blouse or dress and can give the garment an antique or couture look. The method for making these loops is as follows:

Make a mark where you want the button to be. Place the button that you are going to use on the centre of this mark and loop the cord (which can be made from strips of rouleau or from purchased cord or ribbon) round the button to calculate the size needed. Cut the loops the needed length and a bit more, tack and then machine stitch into place (see 5:28). Place the facing on the right side and with both right sides together stitch through the three layers. Trim the seams and turn onto the right side. An additional line of stitching 5 mm from the edge will make the seam lie flat.

Knot buttons

Another way to create individual style in fastening is to make your own Chinese Button Balls which, although they look rather fiddly, are really quite simple to make from tubes of rouleau or from bought cording. They have been used for centuries on Chinese garments such as Dragon Robes. The method for making them is as follows:

Make a piece of rouleau tubing approximately 40 cm long. Holding 5 cm in the left hand make a long loop over the tubing going anticlockwise (5:29). Holding this loop with the left hand, make a second loop and place it underneath the first (5:30). Holding both loops with the left hand, make a third loop which will weave its way through the first and second loop (5:31). When you have these three loops, pull them tight and you will have a ball button (5:32). Make sure that the loops tighten evenly and then cut of any ends that you do not want, remembering to leave approximately 3 cm at each end which will be fastened to the garment. Hand sew the ends on the fabric then wrap some of your sewing threads round these ends to make a shank. The button will now stand up in a decorative way. These buttons can look equally attractive small or large and are generally best used with rouleau loops.

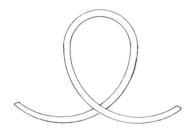

5:29 to 5:32 Chinese buttons.

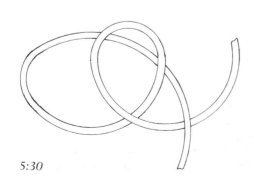

5:30

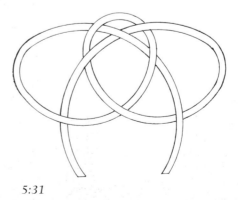

5:31

5:32

Edges with inset fabric shapes

One interesting way of adding visual appeal to garments and to furnishings is to sew extra pieces of fabric on the outer edges of collars, round necklines, on the edges of cushions, etc. These pieces are inset into the seam and, if they are interesting shapes, stand out from the main part of the dress or cushion. Lightweight silk, cotton or polyester are ideal for these shapes which can be made in the same fabric as the dress or cushion or a contrasting one.

One of the simplest ways of creating this effect is to use squares of fabric which have been folded diagonally twice to make triangles (5:33 and 5:34). The fabric must obviously be thin enough so that the layers can be pressed flat and raw edges easily stitched into the seams.

The triangles of silk shantung started as spray dyed strips of fabric which were cut up into 10 cm squares and then folded to give the desired colour effect. I wanted to get maximum contrast of tone between one side of the triangle and the other so the squares were folded accordingly. The advantage of this method of creating decoration is that you make each triangle separately and can therefore experiment with the arrangement of the triangles. The size of triangle can vary: for a decorative neckline, for instance, a folded 5 cm square is probably sufficient. Shapes can be placed side by side or they can overlap. The position in the final seam of the folds in the triangular shapes can vary.

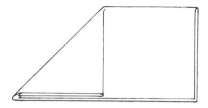

5:33 Fold square of fabric in half. Bring down one end of the folded edge as shown . . .

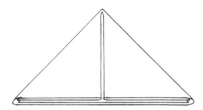

5:34 . . . and then the other end.

Decorative neckline shapes

Another way of making an eye-catching neckline is to make it an interesting shape (5:35). The edge of the neckline has been further decorated with beads and further rows of beads have been added across the centre front and at the side of the bodice. The way to make this kind of neckline is as follows:

Take a piece of paper big enough to fit the whole neckline. Fold it in half. Draw the shape you want on the top half of the paper and then cut

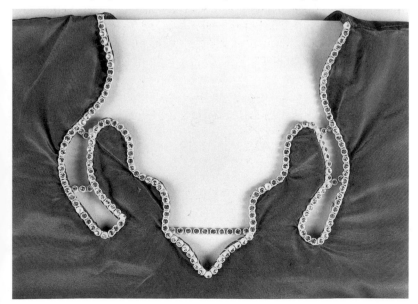

5:35 Shaped neckline edged with glass beads by Shahnaz Aslam.

through the two layers. Remember that it is easier to sew curves than points so do not make your shape too angular. Cut the neckline of your dress the shape of the paper remembering to allow 1.5 cm extra for a seam allowance. Cut a piece from the dress fabric to make a facing of approximately 5 cm wide. It is a good idea to back the facing with a mediumweight iron-on Vilene to give the fabric more stability if the fabric itself is silky. Join the facing and the dress with right sides together, tack and sew together. Clip the seams at regular intervals, turn the facing to the wrong side and press the fabric.

5:36 Brown quilted and shaped yoke by Shahnaz Aslam.

Smocking

Smocking is a way of reducing fullness in a decorative way. The traditional British smock was originally a shift or chemise but by the eighteenth century had evolved as the general overgarment worn by rural working men. Embroidered smocks from this time were made of natural or bleached linen and embroidered by women for family use but were occasionally sold at country fairs. The shape of the smocks was fairly simple but varied according to the occupation of the wearer. The decoration which was added to the smocked areas of the garment consisted of surface embroidery – chain stitches, feather stitches, French knots, etc. Certain embroidery stitches were local and some related to the occupation of the wearer.

In the later nineteenth century the Arts and Crafts movement made the smock fashionable and it was sold ready made (5:37). More recently there has been revival of hand made embroidered smocks, particularly for children.

5:37 Smocked dress (Platt Hall Museum).

5:38 Smocked dress by
Kathleen Cadle.

The smock featured in *5:38* was designed and made by Kathleen Cadle
from Bolton and is a modern version of an old smock which features
embroidered emblems which relate to the area of Bolton. She has used the
emblems of a shuttle and cotton beams on either side of the main body of
the smock to represent Bolton as a historic cotton spinning town. The
buttons are Dorset buttons worked with the red rose of Lancashire. Other
traditional emblems of the area – octagon, the elephant and castle – also
appear. The bee which is a symbol of Manchester is featured on the left
cuff.

Projects

Ruched cushions
The ruched cushions which feature in *Plate 25* were made from lightweight polyester satin in pink which was transfer dyed for the coloured
areas, pink polyester ribbon was appliquéed and the piped edges were
made with pink polyester satin bias binding.

Materials
75 cm pink satin polyester
2 m toning satin bias binding approx.
2 m piping cord
zip measuring 35 cm
threads to match
3 m narrow pink satin ribbon approx.

Method
To make the central square which measures 10×10 cm, cut a piece of
pink fabric measuring 15×15 cm and cut a piece of white paper the same
size – typing or A4 file paper is fine for this – if you use a slightly heavier
weight paper such as cartridge paper the colours will be slightly softer.
Dilute the dyes on a palette till they appear as pastel shades (they will
appear much darker on the actual fabric). For each cushion I used five
colours: diluted violet, pink, yellow, green and blue. Paint the colours on
the paper in a random manner creating a fair amount of interesting juxta-
position and contrast. When colours are dry, lay the paper colour side
down, on the fabric and press with a warm to hot iron – be very careful not
to touch the fabric with a hot iron as it can shrivel. When you have the
depth of colour you want cut a piece of backing fabric for the ruched area
measuring approximately 2 cm more than the square that you want to
make. Mark this square onto the backing fabric with a fabric marker pen
or pencil. Sew the polyester fabric onto the backing, gathering it from time
to time to fit the square. Proceed round all four sides and then with an
appropriate coloured thread (I used embroidery coloured thread for this)
catch the fabric down every so often, letting the material fall into an
interesting pattern. When this has been sewn down securely, cut four
strips of pink fabric and four strips of paper the same size. Paint each piece
of paper with diluted green; try to make it as varied as possible by painting
it darker at one end than at the other; add a touch of pink or any other
colour. Transfer the colour from the paper to the fabric using a hot iron.
Then iron onto each piece of polyester a piece of Vilene the same size. This
stablizes the fabric and makes it easier to work with. With 1.5 cm seam
allowance sew the strips onto the backing fabric and over the edge of the
ruched square. Mitre the corners. Then sew the entire square onto the
plain pink polyester square.

  To finish the cushion you will first need to attach the piping round the
edge of the cushion. It is easy to buy polyester satin bias binding for this but
you can use your own material as long as it is cut on the cross. The piping
cord is inserted into the satin bias binding and this is sewn with the zipper
foot on a sewing machine as close as possible to the cord itself (*5:39*). The
cord encased in the satin bias binding is then tacked and sewn to the right
side of the cushion. Illus. *5:40* shows how to join the cord by unravelling
some of its threads and then rewinding them together and sewing them by
hand to make sure that they are secure.

  Cut two pieces of fabric measuring 22×22 cm for the back of the
cushion. This will allow an ample central back seam to put the zip into.
Mark the length of the zip (in this case 35 cm) leaving an even amount of
2.5 cm at each end. Machine stitch these short seams (*5:41*). Press the

seams open together with the seam allowance on the unsewn opening (5:42). Centre the zip against the opening (5:43). Tack into place and then, using a zipper foot, machine sew the zip into place (5:44).

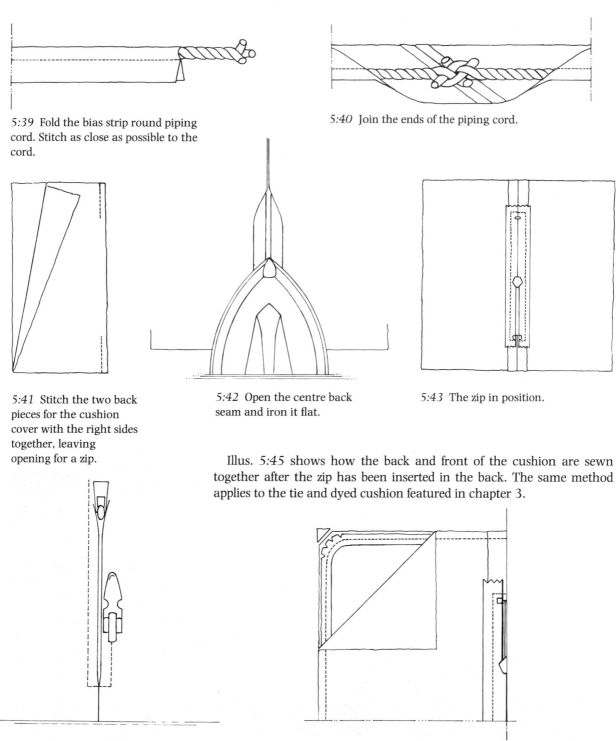

5:39 Fold the bias strip round piping cord. Stitch as close as possible to the cord.

5:40 Join the ends of the piping cord.

5:41 Stitch the two back pieces for the cushion cover with the right sides together, leaving opening for a zip.

5:42 Open the centre back seam and iron it flat.

5:43 The zip in position.

Illus. 5:45 shows how the back and front of the cushion are sewn together after the zip has been inserted in the back. The same method applies to the tie and dyed cushion featured in chapter 3.

5:44 Sew in the zip.

5:45 Sandwich the piping between the front and back of the cushion cover.

6 Designing for textiles

Design inspiration can come from many and varied sources: the world of nature, flowers, trees, fruit, vegetables, animals, fish, insects or birds; history – antique textiles themselves, costumes in museums, rugs, carpets, shawls, embroidered vestments, or domestic agricultural and industrial artifacts; the arts – painting, sculpture, ceramics or jewellry (the colours of the Impressionists, for example, the quality of light in Venetian paintings, the exquisite detailing in Indian Moghul, paintings, stone carving found in rock caves and temple architecture, the dynamic dance of shapes in a Paul Klee).

Buildings and their sculptural features can also be an interesting starting point. Look at decorative stonework arches, columns, copper domes, wrought ironwork, frescoes, roof tiles, stained glass, vaulted ceilings, wood carving and patterns made by decorative brickwork.

It is particularly stimulating to study styles of design from all over the world. For example, look at the complicated motifs in Chinese Mandarin robes, the use of space and density in Japanese prints, the geometric motifs found in ancient Peruvian textiles, the fascinating variety of patterns found in American patchwork quilts, the complex intertwining motifs of Celtic art.

6:1 Mosaic floor at Leighton House, London.

6:2 Victorian tiled building in Westminster, London.

Designing from photographs

Photographs provide an easy source of inspiration which can be directly explored to create an infinite variety of design.

Illus. *6:3* is of birds on land and in flight. The bird at the centre of the photograph already creates an abstract shape. This simple wedge shaped motif has been repeated four times within a circle to form a pendant shaped design (*6:4*). This could be used to make a badge for the back of a jacket, on a bag or for the front of a cushion.

6:3 Wild fowl in Regent's Park, London.

6:4 Design for textiles based on wedge shape.

The photograph of arches *6:5* leads to a continuous and unfolding pattern, resembling a contour design, not dissimilar in character to mola making. The basic linear qualities of these arches have been stylized and treated in perspective to create a design (*6:6*).

6:5 Arcade in the Place des Vosges, Paris.

6:6 Design for textiles based on arches.

The wrought iron Art Nouveau balcony *6:7* consists of stylized foliage. This design can be literally translated into a single motif or repeat design (*6:8*).

6:7 Art Nouveau balcony, Berlin.

6:8 Design for textiles based on cast-iron flowers.

Enlarging designs

Enlarging a sketch to the correct proportions can be done in a number of ways. The drawing can be sub divided into a grid pattern then scaled up on a sheet of paper with a larger grid pattern on it, or on graph paper which had pre-drawn lines on it. Other methods of enlarging designs include projecting the design onto the wall with an overhead projector or with a slide projector (if you have a slide of your image). Remember to select a big enough sheet of paper to hold against the wall so that you can trace a design of the size you wish. A Grant enlarger and photocopier can also be used.

Suppliers

UK

Art Express, 12–20 Westfield Road, Leeds, West Yorkshire
freephone 0800 7414185
dyes, brushes, paper, specialist silk painting products, gutta resist, batik wax

Candle Makers Supplies, 28 Blythe Road, London W14 0HA
tel 020 7602 4031
wax; wax pots, tjantings; Procion M, vat, Dylon and Deka dyes; batik frames

George Weil Textile Craft Supplies, Old Portsmouth Road, Peasmarsh, Guildford, Surrey GU3 1LZ
tel 01483 565800
fabrics, silk paints, gutta, dyes, batik wax, wax pots, tjantings

Hobby Craft Art and Craft Super Store – regional branches
shisha mirrors, embroidery threads, fabric, dyes and paints

John Lewis Partnerships
fabrics, silk paints, gutta, embroidery threads and equipment

Kemtex, Tameside Business Centre, Windmill Lane, Denton, Manchester M34 3QS
tel 0161 320 6505
dyes for cotton, rayon, linen, wool and silk

Silken Strands, 20 Y Rhos, Bangor, Wales LL57 2LT
tel/fax 01248 362 361
shisha mirrors, embroidery materials and equipment

Suasion Ltd, 35 Riding House Street, London W1P 7PT
tel 020 7580 3763
silks, silk paints, gutta, dyes, batik wax, wax pots, tjantings, batik funnel pen

Whalleys (Bradford) Ltd, Harris Court Mills, Great Horton Road, Bradford, West Yorkshire BD7 4EQ
fabrics (silk, cotton, calico, etc.)

Wolfin Textile Ltd, 64 Great Titchfield Street, London W1P 7AE
tel 020 7636 4949   fax 020 7580 4724
basic fabrics

World Embroidery Suppliers, 2 The Woodlands, Kirby Misperton,
Malton, North Yorkshire
tel 01653 668419
shisha mirrors, beads, embroidery threads, fabric

Some Indian and Pakistani clothes shops sell shisha mirrors.

USA

American Art Clay Company, Indianapolis, Indiana
800-374-1600

Artcraft, Norcross, Georgia
800-241-7880

Art Supplies Wholesale, Beverly, Massachusetts
800-462-2420

Blueprints-Printable, Burlingame, California
800-356-0445

FM Brush, Glendale, New York
718-821-5939

Nasco Arts & Crafts, Modesto, California
800-558-9595

Pearl Paint Co, Inc., New York, New York
212-431-7932

Rit Dye, Coventry, Connecticut
317-231-8044

Silkpaint Co., Waldron, Missouri
800-563-0074

Museum Collections

UK

Ashmolean Museum, Oxford
Bankfield Museum, Halifax: Indian, African and Indonesian textiles
Bolton Museum, Lancashire: Egyptian, Coptic, Palestinian and Peruvian
    textiles
Bristol Museum and Art Gallery: Oriental and ethnographic textiles
British Museum, Department of Ethnography, London
British Museum, Department of Oriental Antiquities, London
Cartwright Hall, Bradford
Commonwealth Institute, London: various exhibitions from parts of
    the Commonwealth
Embroiderers Guild, Hampton Court Palace, Hampton Court, Surrey
Fitzwilliam Museum, Cambridge: Turkish, Greek Island and Oriental
    textiles
Horniman Museum, London: ethnographic textiles
Manchester University Museum: ethnographic textiles
Nottingham Museum of Costume and Textiles, Nottingham
Pitt Rivers Museum, Oxford: ethnography
Rochdale Museum, Lancashire: large collection of Indian textiles
Royal Scottish Museum, Edinburgh: large ethnography section
University Museum of Archaeology and Ethnology, Cambridge
Victoria and Albert Museum, London: large textile and costume
    collection from all over the world
Whitworth Museum, Manchester: textiles from all over the world

Canada

Royal Ontario Museum, Toronto, Ontario
National Museum of Mankind, Ottawa, Ontario
Museum of Fine Arts, Montreal

United States

Museum of New Mexico, Santa Fe, New Mexico
Metropolitan Museum of Art, New York
Brooklyn Museum, New York
National Museum of the American Indian, New York
National Museum of Natural History, Smithsonian Institution,
    Washington DC
Philadelphia Museum, Philadelphia, PA
Los Angeles County Museum of Art, Los Angeles
Museum of Cultural History, Los Angeles
Peabody Museum of Archaeology, Cambridge, Massachusetts
Field Museum of Natural History, Chicago
Historic Costume and Textile Collections, University of Washington,
    Seattle, WA

Bibliography

Janet Allen, *Colour Craft*, Hamlyn 1980

E. Anderson, *Tie Dyeing and Batik*, Octopus Books

J. Ayler, *Oriental Costume*, Studio Vista 1974

J. Bhushan, *Costumes and Textiles of India*, F. Lewis Publishers

Marjorie Bowen, *Designing with Dye Resists, Batik and Tie and Dye*, Stephen Hope 1974

Guy Brett, *Through Our Own Eyes*, Gay Men Press 1986

Moira Broadbent, *Animal Regalia*, Portia Press 1985

Jean Cook, *Costumes and Clothes*, Wayland 1986

Esther Dendel, *African Fabric Crafts: sources of African design and technique*, David & Charles 1975 (Taplinger 1974)

Lynda Flower, *Ideas and Techniques for Fabric Design*, Longman 1986

Mary Gostelow, *Embroidery: traditional designs, techniques and patterns from all over the world*, Marshall Cavendish

Peggie Hayden, *The Complete Dressmaker*, Marshall Cavendish 1976

D. Heathcote, *The Arts of the Hausa*, World of Islam Festival Publishing 1976

June Hobson, *Batik Fabrics*, Reeves Dryad 1974

J. Irwin and V. Murphy, *Batiks*, Victoria and Albert Museum 1969

Louise Jefferson, *The Decorative Arts of Africa*, Collins 1974

Jack Lenor Larsen, *The Dyer's Art: ikat, plangi and batik*, Van Nostrand Reinhold 1976

Kersten Lokrantz, *Simple Clothes and How to Make Them* (traditional clothes from all over the world), Penguin 1978

Anne Maile, *Tie and Dye as a Present Day Craft*, Mills & Boon 1963

Dona Z. Meilach, *Contemporary Batik and Tie Dye*, Allen & Unwin 1973

Frederick Palmer, *Themes and Projects in Art and Design*, Longman

Herta Puls, *The Art of Cutwork and Appliqué*, Batsford

John Picton and John Mack, *African Textiles: looms, weaving and design*, British Museum Publications 1979

C. Poliakoff, *African Textiles and Dyeing Techniques*, Routledge

Julia Robinson, *The Penguin Book of Sewing*, Penguin 1974

Renee Robinson, *Fashion Sewing*, Studio Vista 1977

Stuart Robinson, *History of Hand Dyed Textiles*, Mills & Boon 1969

Stuart and Patricia Robinson, *Exploring Fabric Printing*, Mills & Boon 1970

Evelyn Samuel, *Introducing Batik*, Batsford 1968

Eirian Short, *Introducing Quilting*, Batsford 1974

Sue Thompson, *Decorative Dressmaking*, David & Charles 1985

C. A. S. Williams, *Outlines of Chinese Symbolism*, Dover

G. Williams, *African Designs from Traditional Sources*, Dover 1971

Other publications

Embroidered Textiles, Sheila Paine, Thames & Hudson 1990

Indigo Textiles Technique and History, Gosta Sandberg A & C Black 1989

Palestinian Embroidery, Shelagh Weir, British Museum

Shire publications produce small inexpensive books on ethnographic subjects such as Bark Cloth, Indonesian Textile Techniques and Textiles of the Cuna Indians.

Traditional Textiles of Central Asia, Janet Harvey, Thames & Hudson 1996

Traditional Indian Textiles, John Gillow & Nicholas Barnard, Thames & Hudson 1991

Traditional Indonesian Textiles, John Gillow & Barry Dawson, Thames & Hudson 1992

Index